Colossians:

Christ Over All; Christ In You

Gary DeLashmutt

Copyright 2016 by Gary DeLashmutt

Visit http://newparadigmpublishing.com/ for bulk orders and author access

International Standard Book Number 978-0-9976057-1-6

NEW PARADIGM

New Paradigm Publishing

Colossians:
Christ Over ALL: Christ In You

Gary Delashmutt

Contents:

Forward

This book is an adaptation of a teaching series on Colossians which I gave in our church in 2014. I typically write four-page outlines in preparation for such teachings, and our church makes these outlines accessible on its website (www.xenos.org). Many have reported that these outlines are helpful for their own study or teaching preparation. I have simply developed these teaching outlines into chapters in the hope that they will be helpful to a wider audience.

I have long loved Colossians as a concise yet profound summary of Paul's message about Jesus and the Christian life. It introduces spiritual seekers to what C. S. Lewis called "mere Christianity." It grounds younger Christians in their faith as they become familiar with its contents. Christian workers will derive lasting nourishment and motivation by memorizing and meditating on specific passages. My hope and prayer is that God will use this little book to open many eyes to the richness of Colossians and to the greatness of the Jesus revealed therein.

Unless otherwise indicated, I have used the *New American Standard Bible* when quoting biblical passages. I have included many additional interpretive comments in the footnotes for the sake of those interested in such matters.

I am grateful to our church, Xenos Christian Fellowship, for the opportunity to teach the Bible over the last four decades. I am also grateful for the many fellow-workers and friends with whom I serve. I am especially grateful to my wife, Bev, who has willingly sacrificed over the years so that I can teach the Bible. Most of all, I am grateful to the Lord for His mercy in allowing me to explain and apply His Word to others.

Not to us, O Lord, not to us, but to your name goes all the glory for your unfailing love and faithfulness. (Psalm 115:1 NLT)

Gary DeLashmutt

Chapter 1
Colossians 1:1-8
Introduction to Colossians

The Setting

Colossians is a letter from Paul, one of the leaders of the early Christian movement, to the Christians who lived in Colossae, a small town in southwestern Turkey. Colossae no longer exists; it was destroyed by an earthquake a few years after Paul wrote this letter.

Paul was a prisoner (probably in Rome) when he wrote this letter (4:3), around 60 AD. He did not start this church; in fact he had never actually visited Colossae (2:1). Some years earlier, Paul had set up a training center in Ephesus. He stayed there for almost three years, using a classroom in the school of Tyrannus to give daily lectures about the kingdom of God (Acts 19:8-10). As a result of Paul's lectures, this message spread all over western Turkey.

A Colossian named Epaphras (4:12), whom Paul evidently trained in Ephesus, came back to his home town and started this church (1:7). Epaphras had recently visited Paul with concerns about the Colossian church, specifically that they were being influenced by pseudo-Christian teachers. Paul wrote this letter primarily to strengthen the Colossian Christians to resist these false teachers (2:4).

> [1:1] Paul, an apostle of Jesus Christ by the will of God, and Timothy our brother,
> [2] to the saints and faithful brethren in Christ who are at Colossae: Grace to you and peace from God our Father. [3] We

give thanks to God, the Father of our Lord Jesus Christ, praying always for you, [4] since we heard of your faith in Christ Jesus and the love which you have for all the saints; [5] because of the hope laid up for you in heaven, of which you previously heard in the word of truth, the gospel, [6] which has come to you, just as in all the world also it is constantly bearing fruit and increasing, even as it has been doing in you also since the day you heard of it and understood the grace of God in truth; [7] just as you learned it from Epaphras, our beloved fellow bond-servant, who is a faithful servant of Christ on our behalf, [8] and he also informed us of your love in the Spirit.

Paul begins by thanking God for this church and for how it got started. He says they are one example of Christian communities that were springing up all over the Roman Empire. He uses an agricultural metaphor to describe what is happening. It's like a tomato plant that germinates from seed, grows and bears fruit, and whose seed then spreads and germinates other plants.

What is the "seed" that caused this growth? It's not Epaphras; Paul says they got the "seed" from him. It wasn't Paul, because he had not been to Colossae. Paul and Epaphras were "seed" agents, but they were not "seeds." The "seed" is what Paul calls "the gospel." It spread (probably) from Paul to Epaphras and from Epaphras to them, and since then it was spreading from them to others in their area.

What is this "gospel?" In our culture, "gospel" refers to several things vaguely related to Christianity—a style of music, a certain kind of preaching, or a religious place ("gospel tabernacle"). But the gospel of which Paul speaks exists independently from these things and is very different from them. Paul uses this term 57 times in his letters, so it is both a content-rich and important term. He says elsewhere that it contains "unfathomable riches" (Ephesians 3:8). This passage provides us with four important insights into the gospel.

#1: The gospel is a definitive announcement

Paul calls the gospel "the word of truth" (1:5), or "the message that is true." In other words, the gospel is not one of many messages, nor is it human speculation; it is *the* message of truth revealed by God for all people. This claim was, and is, counter-cultural. First-century Roman culture, like twenty-first century American culture, advocated religious syncretism, or "cafeteria" spirituality – taking bits of different religious systems and mixing them according to personal preference. Such religious pragmatism is fraught with intellectual problems, including lack of objective evidence and logical contradiction. But the gospel claims to be the ultimate revelation of God to humans, confirmed by historical events and logically consistent.

In referring to this message, Paul was using a word with which his audiences were already familiar. The Greek word is *euaggelion*, which means "good message." Roman rulers used this word to describe certain official and definitive announcements. Specifically, a Roman "gospel" announced an important event and summoned people to align their lives to this event. For example, during Caesar Augustus' reign (9 BC), a provincial assembly in Asia Minor proclaimed the "gospel" of Caesar's uniquely peaceful reign and summoned all subjects to reckon time from a new calendar based on his birthday:

> "Whereas the Providence... has brought our life to the peak of perfection in giving to us Augustus Caesar... and who, being sent to us and to our descendants as a savior, has put an end to war and has set all things in order; and... whereas... the birthday of the god (Caesar Augustus) *has been for the whole world the beginning of the gospel*

(*euaggelion*) *concerning him,* therefore, let all reckon a new era beginning from the date of his birth."[1]

Most Romans knew that this "gospel" of Caesar Augustus was overblown. The philosopher Epictetus, wrote: "While the emperor may give peace from war on land and sea, he is unable to give peace from passion, grief, and envy. He cannot give peace of heart, for which man yearns more than even for outward peace."[2]

While Caesar Augustus ended war within the Empire, he fell far short of "setting all things in order," let alone bringing "life to the peak of perfection." The Empire was still riddled with racial, socio-economic and gender divisions. People lamented that true peace of mind and heart were as out of reach as ever. Not much has changed since then!

It is in this context that the early Christian movement announced a greater gospel. This gospel announced the coming of a much greater Ruler who has brought a much greater salvation.

#2: The gospel declares that Jesus is the Christ

Who is this greater Ruler? It is Jesus, of course. The gospel must be centrally about Jesus, because Paul speaks of Jesus five times in these eight verses. Elsewhere, he calls the gospel "the gospel concerning our Lord Jesus" (2 Thessalonians 1:8).[3]

Specifically, the gospel declares that Jesus is the Christ. "Jesus" refers to Jesus of Nazareth, the Jewish carpenter, born around 4 BC and crucified by Roman rulers in 33 AD. Paul calls Him "Jesus Christ"

---

[1] The Priene Inscription (9 BC), included in Wilhemus Dittenberger, *Orientis Graeci Inscriptiones Selectae* (1905).

[2] Cited in Norval Geldenhuys, *Commentary on the Gospel of Luke* (Eerdmans, 1972), p.112

[3] Paul also calls the gospel "the gospel of God's Son" (Romans 1:9) and "the gospel of Christ" (Romans 15:19; 1 Corinthians 9:12; 2 Corinthians 2:12; 9:13; 10:14; Galatians 1:7; 1 Thessalonians 3:2).

(1:1), "Christ" (1:2), "our Lord Jesus Christ" (1:3), "Christ Jesus" (1:4), and "Christ" (1:7). "Christ" is not Jesus' last name, any more than "H" is His middle initial. "Christ" is His *title*. The Greek "Christos" was the equivalent for the Hebrew word "Messiah" – the One predicted by the Old Testament prophets, the coming rightful Ruler of the whole world. That's why Paul also calls Jesus "Lord." Because the gospel declares that Jesus (not Caesar or any human ruler) is the Christ and the Lord, it was (and is) an extremely counter-cultural message!

The gospel declares not that Jesus *was* the Christ, but that Jesus *is* the Christ. Jesus didn't just die; He also rose from the dead and is forever alive. That's why these verses speak of Jesus as a living Ruler who is personally accessible even though He had been crucified over 25 years earlier. Paul is an apostle (ambassador) of the *living* Jesus, and Epaphras is a servant of the *living* Christ. The gospel is not simply a historical record that preserves the memory of Jesus; it is an invitation to meet Him and serve Him.

#3: The gospel offers the grace of God

What is the greater salvation that Jesus brought? Paul tells us by using another synonym for the gospel in 1:6 – "the grace of God in truth," or "the truth about God's grace." Paul says in Colossians chapters 1 and 2 that Jesus' death on the cross made it possible for God to offer His grace to people like us who deserve His judgment. "Grace" (*charis*) means "a free and undeserved gift." It is the root of our word "charity," which is a free gift of aid to people who are unable to earn it for themselves. Elsewhere (Acts 20:24), Paul calls the gospel "the gospel concerning God's grace."

This passage identifies several aspects of God's grace:

- True peace (1:2b). Paul begins almost all of his letters with the salutation: "Grace and peace to you through Jesus Christ." The order is very important because it is receiving

God's grace that leads to peace. There are three types of
peace you can experience from God's grace. First, peace with
God which delivers you from His judgment and makes Him
your loving Father (Romans 5:1). Second, peace within your
soul regardless of your circumstances because God's fatherly
care can now guard your heart and mind from anxiety
(Philippians 4:6-7). Finally, it enables you to live in peace
with other brothers and sisters in Christ (Ephesians 4:3).

- Hope (1:4-5). No longer do you have to fear the future or
  your death. The moment you put your faith in Jesus, God
  guarantees that you will spend eternity with Him (1:4). Hope
  is the confident expectation that this future is "laid up for
  you in heaven." Paul is simply restating what Jesus said in
  John 3:16 – "For God so loved the world, that He gave His
  only begotten Son, that whoever believes in Him should not
  perish, but have eternal life."

- The ability to love others. There are two reasons why God's
  grace gives us this ability. First, the certainty of eternal life
  provides you with a basis for spending this life giving to
  people instead of taking from them or protecting yourself
  from them. It is "*because of* the hope laid up for you in
  heaven (1:5) that you can have "love for all the saints" (1:4).
  An old beer jingle said: "You only go around once in life, so
  grab for all the gusto you can." This temporal philosophy of
  life leads to self-centered relating – which leads to failure in
  our relationships. But Paul says: "You're going to live forever,
  so give all the love you can." When we relate to one another
  out of the fullness of God's eternal love for us, we can
  become givers rather than takers. Second, God's Spirit
  indwells you the moment you put your faith in Jesus (1:8).
  His Spirit enables you to personally experience Jesus' love

(Romans 5:5) and He provides motivation and power to give Jesus' love to others (Philippians 2:13).

We're going to learn much more about the gospel of God's grace in Colossians. But if these were its only provisions, this is an amazing offer! Who does not want peace, hope, and the ability to really love others? You don't have to wait until some distant time in the future to receive this gift; you can receive it today. You don't have to clean yourself up first or perform special religious observances; you can receive this gift just the way you are. The living Jesus is offering you God's grace, and the only condition is that you entrust yourself to Him as your Savior and Lord (1:4).

#4: The gospel spreads through people who have been changed by it

I know people who have learned about the gospel by reading the Bible alone. I know people who learned about the gospel from history professors who didn't believe it. But the main way the gospel spreads is from person to person.

The Colossians learned about the gospel through Epaphras, who had been changed by it (1:6-7). We don't know how Epaphras learned about the gospel. Maybe he left small-town Colossae for the "big city" of Ephesus to fulfill his dreams, but got bitterly disappointed. Then perhaps he met some Christians who had real peace and hope and love—and they explained the gospel to him. Maybe they also asked him to come listen to Paul teach about the gospel.

However Epaphras heard the gospel, when he put his faith in Jesus, he too began to experience this same peace and hope and love. No wonder he came back to Colossae and shared the gospel with his friends and family! The "seed" came through Epaphras, and when they heard the gospel and saw how it had changed him, some of them decided: "I want what Epaphras has!" Then they experienced the same peace, hope, and love, and then they started telling people they knew, and so on.

This is the main way the gospel spread all over the Roman Empire during the first century – from 500 Jews in 33 AD to a million people from many ethnic backgrounds by the end of the century, reaching as far east as India, as far north as Great Britain, as far west as Spain, and as far south as northern Africa. The gospel spread as an underground, grassroots movement, mainly through people whose names we will never know until we meet them in heaven.

This is the main way the gospel is still spreading today. Did you receive Christ because you heard the gospel from people who had been changed by it? I did. Two of my fellow drug-using friends met Jesus and experienced His transforming grace. They weren't knowledgeable in the Bible; they didn't know sophisticated arguments for Christianity. They simply told me that Jesus was real and that He had changed their lives – and they urged me to ask Him into my heart so I could experience the same change. I argued with them and mocked them, but when I hit a wall, what they said came forcefully to my mind. I thought, "I know there has been a change in them, and I want that change. If they say it comes from receiving Jesus, I'm going to find out if it's true." So I just called out silently and said, "Jesus, I want you to come into my life and show me that you are real. If you will do this, I will follow you." The "seed" of the gospel germinated in my heart at that moment, and it has been changing me ever since!

Have you met Jesus and been changed by His grace? Then you are fully qualified to spread this gospel to others! You don't have to possess extensive biblical knowledge. You don't have to be free from all your sins and problems. You don't have to be a gifted public speaker. You don't have to be able to answer every question or objection. The gospel message, coupled with your testimony of its impact on your life, has the power to germinate in any receptive heart. So don't worry about what you *don't* know; share what you *do* know whenever you get the opportunity. Just put it out there like my friends did, and invite people to encounter the living Jesus for themselves! This kind of "abundant sowing" will eventually lead to an abundant harvest!

Chapter 2
Colossians 1:9-12
Spiritual Transformation

As we saw in the previous chapter, Paul begins his letter to the Colossians by thanking God that they had received the "gospel." The gospel is the message that Jesus is the one true King and that His death purchases God's complete salvation for all who entrust themselves to Him. Paul also rejoices that this gospel had begun to change their lives, imparting a guarantee of eternal life that motivates genuine love for others.

Now, in the next paragraph, Paul describes his ongoing prayer for them since he heard of their conversion.

> [1.9] For this reason also, since the day we heard of it, we have not ceased to pray for you and to ask that you may be filled with the knowledge of His will in all spiritual wisdom and understanding, [10] so that you will walk in a manner worthy of the Lord, to please Him in all respects, bearing fruit in every good work and increasing in the knowledge of God; [11] strengthened with all power, according to His glorious might, for the attaining of all steadfastness and patience; joyously [12] giving thanks to the Father, who has qualified us to share in the inheritance of the saints in Light.

Paul prays that God would change their lives in a deep and lasting way. Elsewhere, Paul calls this change being "transformed" (Romans 12:2; 2 Corinthians 3:18). The Greek verb is *metamorphoo*, from which we get our word "metamorphosis." It means "to be changed into another form," or to be changed from the inside-out. Think of how a caterpillar metamorphoses into a butterfly.

When Jesus returns, He will completely and perfectly transform all who believe in Him – even to the extent of giving glorious new bodies like His resurrected body. (Colossians 3:4; see also Romans 8:23; 1 John 3:2)

In the meantime, Jesus' Spirit is ceaselessly at work in this life to transform our characters. Paul provides a description of this transformation in 1:10-12; he explains how God effects this transformation in 1:9b.

A description of spiritual transformation

Paul describes the central goal of God's transformation in 1:10a – "...so that you will walk in a manner worthy of the Lord, to please Him in all respects..." "Worthy of the Lord" doesn't mean "deserving God's acceptance." We already have God's complete and permanent acceptance through Christ from the moment we believe in Him. Rather, it means living in a way that accurately represents God to others, so that we enhance His reputation and attract others to Him. "To please Him in all respects" means the same thing, because the life that enhances God's reputation *is* the life that pleases Him.

 We receive here two basic insights into spiritual transformation, both of which are deeply counter-cultural:

- First, God wants to transform us from self-centered people into God-centered people. God's transformation seeks to fundamentally displace us as the center of our worlds, and to enable us to orbit around Him and His will, to "please Him." This is radically different from most contemporary forms of spirituality, which view God as a force or energy or genie we use to facilitate our self-chosen goals.

- Second, God wants our transformation to be comprehensive, not compartmentalized. His transformation seeks to realign our lives to His will "in all respects." This is fundamentally different from most contemporary forms of spirituality, which seek change in certain self-chosen areas (such as emotional healing), while declaring other areas (such as sexual behavior or finances) off-limits. Later, Paul will show how God wants to transform us in every area of our lives: intellectual, sexual, financial, relational, marital, parental, career, etc.

You may be thinking at this point: "This transformation would make me miserable!" But you are mistaken, because God *designed* us for this way of life. It is living in contradiction to His design that damages us and brings misery to us and others. Allowing God to transform us to live according to His design brings deep fulfillment. As Paul says elsewhere:

> Do not be conformed to this world, but be transformed by the renewing of your mind, so that you may prove what the will of God is, that which is *good* and *well-pleasing* and *perfect.* (Romans 12:2)

Do you want more specifics concerning this transformed way of life? Paul provides a four-fold snap-shot of it in Colossians 1:10b-12:

> 1:10 ... *bearing fruit* in every good work and *increasing* in the knowledge of God;
> 11 *strengthened* with all power, according to His glorious might, for the attaining of all steadfastness and patience; joyously 12 *giving thanks* to the Father, who has qualified us to share in the inheritance of the saints in Light.

- *"Bearing fruit in every good work"* – "Good work" does not refer to doing religious deeds to earn God's acceptance or to impress other people. It refers rather to a life of active loving goodness

that attracts others to Christ. Paul used the same phrase
("bearing fruit") in this sense in 1:6.

Many activities can provide us with a temporary burst of joy. But
nothing is more deeply satisfying than having God work through
you to influence others toward Him! This is what Jesus promised His
followers who "bear fruit" for Him:

> "My Father is glorified by this, that you bear much fruit, and so
> prove to be My disciples... These things I have spoken to you so
> that My joy may be in you, and that your joy may be made full."
> (John 15:8,11)

- *Increasing in the knowledge of God"* – This "knowledge of God"
  involves learning and affirming biblical truths about who God is.
  But "knowledge" here refers also to experiential, personal
  knowledge – a growing personal intimacy with God. As you
  experience God's love through Jesus and then follow Him in
  giving His love away to others, He grants you even deeper
  disclosure of His love (see John 14:21,23). And since God is
  infinite, we can keep growing in our knowledge of His love
  throughout this life and then through all eternity (see
  Ephesians 2:7)!

- *"Being strengthened with all power according to His glorious
  might...."* – You might expect this phrase to end with "...so that
  you may perform miracles" or "so that you may see visions." Paul
  experienced the power of God in both of these ways, and you
  might also. But these things are not the greatest manifestations of
  God's power. God's transforming power enables you to become
  "steadfast" (able to hang in there through difficult circumstances
  that formerly crushed you), and to become "patient" (able to
  keep loving difficult people whom you formerly gave up on or
  rejected). As a result, you can be realistic about how tough this

life is, and yet become increasingly stable and faithful – an
amazing transformation indeed!

- *"Joyously giving thanks to the Father..."* – We all know people
who stick out life's difficulties stoically or cynically, but God's
transformation leads to a life of steadfastness and patience
infused with joy and gratitude. Why? Because through Jesus,
God has become our loving Father and has bestowed on us the
privileged status of being His beloved children. One day we will
inherit a place in His eternal kingdom, and in the meantime we
can come to Him for whatever help we need. All this is ours,
despite the fact that we deserve to be condemned for our many
sins! The more we contemplate this amazing provision, the more
grateful and joyful we become!

No matter how much you've messed your life up, no matter how
much others have mistreated you, no matter how difficult your
current circumstances are, God has the power to transform you in
this direction. If you have received Christ, He has staked His
reputation on you, and He is totally committed to attracting other
people to Himself through your changed life!

How God transforms us

Paul describes how God transforms us in 1:9.

> [1:9]... we have not ceased to pray for you and to ask that you
> may be filled with the knowledge of His will in all spiritual
> wisdom and understanding [10] *so that* you will walk in a
> manner worthy of the Lord...

Being "filled with the knowledge of God's will in all spiritual wisdom
and understanding" unleashes God's power to transform our lives.
Many Christians think that "the knowledge of God's will" refers to
getting God's guidance for important life decisions such as who to
marry, where to go to school, or what career to pursue. These

decisions are important, and God can give us guidance on how to make them. But that is not what Paul is talking about. Rather, "the knowledge of God's will in all spiritual wisdom" is a synonym for the gospel – that Jesus is the Messiah, and that His death and resurrection has provided the solution to our deepest problems.[1] Paul makes this clear in 2:2b-3, where he speaks of the "true knowledge of God's mystery, that is, Christ Himself, in whom are hidden all the treasures of wisdom and knowledge."

So the key to being transformed by God is the same thing that is the key to becoming a Christian and experiencing God's peace and hope (see Chapter 1) – understanding and internalizing the content of the gospel. The difference is that becoming a Christian requires only a basic understanding of the gospel (i.e., that Jesus died for your sins and wants to live in your heart), while being deeply transformed by God requires being "filled" with a deeper and more comprehensive understanding of the gospel. How do you become filled with this knowledge? We will explore Paul's many answers to this question in subsequent chapters. By way of overview, consider these three ways of increasing your knowledge of the gospel:

- First, *become deeply familiar with the contents of the gospel.* It is precisely this knowledge that Paul communicates in the next section of this letter, which we will explore in later chapters.[2] Then he explicitly calls the Colossians (and us) to "Let the word of Christ richly dwell within you" (3:16a). Paul is saying: "Listen carefully to what I have taught you about the gospel. Become so familiar with its contents that it is at thoroughly home in your soul." This kind of in-depth familiarity could include committing to memory whole

---

[1] Paul refers to this message as "the mystery of God's will" in Eph. 1:9, and calls it "the *gospel* of your salvation" in Eph. 1:13.

[2] See especially Paul's teaching about who Jesus is (1:15-20), what He accomplished through His death on the cross (2:10-15), and Paul's statement in 3:1-4.

passages of this letter so that you can recall and ponder them frequently. This is what the Colossian Christians would have done, since they would have been unable to possess their own copies of Paul's letter.

By contrast, most American Christians, while having access to multiple translations of the New Testament, have only a cursory understanding of the gospel – and therefore remain needlessly in a state of spiritual immaturity.

- Second, *ask God to illuminate the gospel's application to your life*. This is why, even as Paul taught the Colossians these truths, he prayed for his readers to be filled with spiritual wisdom and understanding (1:9). God's Spirit enables you to "know the things freely given to us by God" (1 Corinthians 2:12). He loves to open the eyes of your heart so that you can see how these truths apply practically to your life. For example, as you read my comments on 1:10,11, perhaps the Spirit ignited in you a fresh longing to be more steadfast in a current, specific adversity. Or perhaps He enlightened you about what it looks like to be more patient in a current difficult relationship. Or perhaps He brought to mind a specific way you can be more actively loving at home or at work. Turn these spiritual insights into prayerful steps of faith. As you do so, God's Spirit will unleash His power to transform your thinking, your character, and your life!

- Third, *take these same steps with other Christians*. In Colossians 2:2, Paul says that it is those who are "knit together in love" that "attain to the wealth that comes from the full assurance of understanding, resulting in a true knowledge of... Christ" "Knit together" (*sumbibazo*) refers to a close and living connection – like the life-sharing connection between the organs in our physical bodies.

Isolated Christians become defeated Christians. But we experience transforming growth as we hold fast to Christ and are supplied by His life through the "joints and ligaments" (2:19) – our brothers and sisters in Christ. This is why we need to teach and counsel "one another" with the Word of Christ (3:16) – regularly studying and discussing and applying God's Word in the context of Christian friendships (see Chapter 4).

Do you want a life that is increasingly characterized by the transformation Paul describes in 1:10-12? God wants to give this to you, and His Spirit is able to provide it for you! Regardless of your circumstances, you can appropriate the Spirit's life-transforming power by building a lifestyle around the above priorities. Why not ask God right now to give you a step to move in this direction?

Chapter 3
Colossians 1:15-23
The "Who" of the Gospel: Jesus

Paul wrote this letter to re-focus the Colossian Christians on what he calls "the gospel." We learned in Chapter 1 that "gospel" was a technical term for the announcement of a world-changing event, coupled with a summons to entrust oneself to this event. The Christian gospel is the announcement that Jesus has come and won the ultimate victory through His death on the cross, and a summons for everyone to entrust themselves to Jesus.

Why does Paul have to re-focus the Colossians on the gospel? Because some pseudo-Christian teachers were saying that the gospel was merely a spiritual "starter kit"—and that the Colossian Christians needed to graduate to other spiritual "secrets" in order to attain spiritual fullness. Paul rejects this proposition, arguing instead that healthy spiritual development depends on continuing to grow in their understanding and appreciation of who Jesus is and what He has provided them through His death.

> $^{2.9}$ For in Him all the fullness of Deity dwells in bodily form, ^{10} and in Him (i.e., through His death on the cross) you have been made complete (full)...

To this end, Paul spends the first half of his letter expounding the meaning of the gospel. He begins by addressing the "Who" of the gospel—Jesus. The identity of Jesus is crucial, because *who Jesus is determines what He can provide for us.* If He is only a lower spirit-being, or only a moral teacher or prophet or model of God-

consciousness—as many claim today—then He can only give us
partial help toward spiritual wholeness. But in Colossians 1:15-20,
Paul recites what may be a poem or song that asserts the absolute
supremacy of Jesus.[1] Then in Colossians 1:21-23, he concisely
summarizes what kind of salvation Jesus has provided for us.

Jesus is absolutely supreme

[1:15] He is the image of the invisible God, the firstborn of all
creation. [16] For by Him all things were created, both in the
heavens and on earth, visible and invisible, whether thrones
or dominions or rulers or authorities—all things have been
created through Him and for Him. [17] He is before all things,
and in Him all things hold together. [18] He is also head of the
body, the church; and He is the beginning, the firstborn
from the dead, so that He Himself will come to have first
place in everything. [19] For it was the Father's good pleasure
for all the fullness to dwell in Him, [20] and through Him to
reconcile all things to Himself, having made peace through
the blood of His cross; through Him, I say, whether things on
earth or things in heaven. (Colossians 1:15-20)

Before we evaluate this description of Jesus more carefully, notice
that Paul uses the word "all" seven times, and that he insists that
Jesus is supreme over "everything." In Ezekiel 1, Ezekiel saw a vision
of angelic beings that are so glorious that he was tempted to worship
them. But then he sees that they are only the "pedestal" of the one

---

[1] The structure of these verses is poem-like or song-like. "The weight of New Testament
scholarly opinion today considers that Colossians 1:15-20 is a pre-Pauline 'hymn' inserted
into the letter's train of thought by the author." P. T. O'Brien, *Colossians, Philemon* (Word,
1998), Vol. 44, p. 32. However, other scholars believe that Paul may have composed this song-
poem himself. "So exactly do these words suit the needs of the Colossians, and so perfectly do
they form a foundation for the rest of this particular letter, that it seems more likely that Paul
is either freely adapting traditional material or constructing with God-given wisdom his own
explanation of the glory of Christ." R. C. Lucas, *Fullness and Freedom: The message of
Colossians and Philemon,* (InterVarsity Press, 1980), p. 45.

true God who towers far above them. Paul is saying that Jesus is not one of the "pedestals"—He is the God who towers above them.

Paul makes three assertions about Jesus' cosmic supremacy in this passage:

- *Jesus is the unique and perfect Revelation of God (1:15a,19).*
  Jesus is not merely an angel/spirit-being, or a prophet, or one of many enlightened spiritual masters. Jesus is *the* image of God—the perfect and definitive revelation of God (see also John 1:18 and Hebrews 1:3). *All* of the *fullness* of God dwells in Him alone.

- *Jesus is the absolute Owner of the entire universe (1:15b-17).* "First-born" in 1:15b does not mean that Jesus was the first created being; it means that Jesus is the rightful heir or owner of the whole universe.[2] 1:16,17 provide four reasons why this is so:

  Jesus is the *means through which the universe was created.* Not only all material objects, but all persons (including all human and angelic rulers) derive their existence from Jesus' creative activity.

  The universe is made *for* Jesus. Only under Jesus' rulership will creation fulfill its ultimate purpose. Otherwise, creation exists in a state of futility (see Romans 8:21,22).

  Jesus *predates* the universe. This follows from Jesus' role in creation. In order to bring the universe into being, He must have existed before it.

---

[2] The Old Testament often uses "first-born" in a non-literal way. For example, God refers to Israel as His "son" or "first-born" (Exodus 4:22). He refers to David as His "first-born, the highest of the kings of the earth" (Psalm 89:27). Since heirs were normally first-born sons, it is easy to see how this term can be used as a synonym for "heir."

Jesus *holds the universe together.* The universe is not an
independently-operating machine. Jesus personally
sustains all created things at all times.

- *Jesus is the sole Redeemer of our broken universe (1:18-20).*
  God's creation (at least on earth) is now broken. Nature is in
  an abnormal state, humans die because of sin, and both
  spiritual and human rulers oppose God. But Jesus has come
  to completely mend this situation. He is not merely one of
  many ways to this mending; He is the only Mender. On the
  cross, He defeated the reason for the brokenness (sin) and
  its ultimate manifestation (death). His physical resurrection
  is the beginning of the eventual healing He will bring to
  nature, humans and the spiritual realm.

When Paul says that Jesus "made peace through the blood of
His cross," he does not mean that all humans and angels will
be ultimately saved. Paul affirms that many will spend
eternity apart from God (2 Thessalonians 1:9). Rather, he
means that Jesus and His death on the cross save every
repentant person (1:18), and establishes Him as the Lord to
whom "every knee shall bow" (Philippians 2:10-11)—
including his unrepentant enemies (1:20). He means that
Jesus will ultimately overcome all opposition to God (both
humans and demonic) when He returns.

It's important to realize that this Jesus is not just "Paul's
Jesus"—the figment of Paul's imagination or some myth he
heard from others. This is the same portrait of the Messiah
that the Old Testament prophets describe and predict. This is
the same claim that Jesus made for Himself. This is the same
Jesus that His original disciples describe. The earliest
Christians suffered and died for this same Jesus; they insisted
that Jesus—not Caesar or any other god—is Lord.

Many people today believe that we cannot know the true identity of Jesus of Nazareth. Some say that Jesus is whoever we believe Him to be. Others say that later church leaders invented or preserved the New Testament's view of Jesus because it advanced their political agendas. But Jesus is not some shadowy, ambiguous historical figure; His historical profile is as clear and sharp as any figure in ancient history. He is not a piece of pliable historical clay that we can mold to our own preferences; He is like a rock-solid statue that we must worship or reject. Our faith doesn't make Jesus who He is; our faith enables us to receive the salvation that only He can provide us. This is what Paul explains in Chapter 1:21-23.

Jesus can save us completely

Because Jesus is God, He can save us completely. Some people (like me at one time) want Jesus to be ambiguous because they are offended at the notion that they need to be saved. But that's what the real Jesus came to do, because that's what we really need. That's why the tone changes abruptly in Colossians 1:21.

> [1, 21] And although you were formerly alienated and hostile in mind, engaged in evil deeds, [22] yet He has now reconciled you in His fleshly body through death, in order to present you before Him holy and blameless and beyond reproach...

The language in 1:15-20 was wide-angle, even cosmic in its scope. Jesus is so big and supreme that we are less than gnats compared to Him. But suddenly, beginning in 1:21, Paul's language changes to up-close-and-personal. This Jesus who is supreme over the whole universe is also the One who loves "you" and came to save "you." Try reading 1:21,22a with "I" and "me" to personalize these verses as Paul intended.

Paul speaks of two different aspects of salvation that Jesus provides
for each of us:

- *Jesus reconciles us to God.* Reconciliation is one of the most
  beautiful words in the New Testament. It means not merely
  the cessation of hostilities (cease-fire); it is the re-
  establishment of a love relationship between two estranged
  persons by resolving the root causes of their conflict. When
  my wife and I were alienated in the early years of our
  marriage, it wasn't enough to merely not scream or slam
  doors. We needed outside help to resolve the root issues and
  really recover loving trust and intimacy.
  Because of our sin and rebellion, we were at enmity with
  God. And because our sin offends this holy God, He was at
  enmity with us.

But such is God's love that He took the initiative by coming in the
Person of Jesus to pay the penalty of our sin, even while we were still
at enmity with Him (Romans 5:8). Through Jesus' death, God is now
ready and willing to embrace us in a love relationship. The moment
we end our rebellion by asking Jesus for His gift of forgiveness, we
become permanently reconciled to God.

What about you? Have you been reconciled to God—or are you still
a fugitive from Him? Are you ready to turn toward God, admit that
you have been a rebel, and then receive the gift of forgiveness that
Jesus purchased through His death? If you insist that you're too good
to need this, your pride will keep you alienated from God. If you
insist on cleaning yourself up before you return to God, your pride
will keep you alienated from God. But if you come as you are—as an
unworthy person—to Jesus, He will reconcile you to God!

- *Jesus transforms our lives.* Jesus reconciles us to God "in
  order to present you before Him holy and blameless and
  beyond reproach" (1:22b). "Holy and blameless and beyond

reproach" is a state we will reach perfectly only when Jesus returns, but Paul seems to use this phrase here as a synonym for spiritual maturity in this life.[3] Jesus wants to not only forgive us of sin's penalty; He wants to heal us from sin's corrupting and damaging power. He wants to "renovate" our lives from the inside out so that we become more and more like the person God created us to be (see Colossians 3:10)—someone who loves God and His ways, and who loves people the way He loves us.

The moment we receive Jesus' reconciliation, He begins this transformation. No other person (no matter how evil) and no circumstance (no matter how adverse) can stop Him from transforming us because Jesus is far more powerful than they are. The only condition is that we stay focused on the gospel:

> If indeed you continue in the faith firmly established and steadfast, and not moved away from the hope of the gospel that you have heard...(Colossians 1:23)

As we stay focused on Jesus and what He has provided us through His death, His Spirit will gradually transform us (see 2 Corinthians 3:18). If we stray from this focus, we will remain reconciled to God, but we will short-circuit His transformation process. Paul is concerned that the Colossians would stray from this focus because of the false teachers' influence. Likewise, we should be careful not to stray from this focus on Jesus and His grace—not only to false views of Jesus, but also to sub-Christian religious practices like those Paul describes in Colossians 2:16-23 (see Chapter 7).

---

[3] Notice that in the following context (Colossians 1:28), Paul speaks of cooperating with God to "present every Christians complete (or mature) in Christ." Paul also uses these adjectives ("holy;" "blameless;" "beyond reproach") in Philippians 2:15 to describe spiritual maturity. This understanding of Colossians 1:22b,23 preserves Paul's assurance that believers in Jesus are eternally secure (see Colossians 2:13,14), while emphasizing that our sanctification (or spiritual growth) is contingent to an ongoing faith-focus on Jesus and the provisions of His grace.

How do we stay focused on the gospel? We looked at Paul's brief answer to this question in Colossians 1:9-12 (Chapter 2), and we will look at his more extensive answer in Colossians 3:1-4 (Chapter 8). If we are correct in assuming that 1:15-20 was an early Christian poem or a song, Paul is providing us with a very practical way to stay focused on the gospel. He urges in Colossians 3:16 to:

> [3, 16] Let the word of Christ richly dwell within you...with psalms and hymns and spiritual songs, singing with thankfulness in your hearts to God.

"The word of Christ" is a synonym for the gospel. Paul's command to "Let the word of Christ richly dwell within you" is a synonym for: "Stay focused on the gospel." So one of the ways we can stay focused on the gospel is by singing spiritual songs about Jesus.

Maybe Paul composed this song while he was imprisoned, and seemingly completely under the control of the Roman emperor, Nero. If so, Paul would have often sung this song during his imprisonment, as he and Silas did while imprisoned in Philippi (see Acts 16:25). It would have reminded him that Jesus is sovereign over Nero, that his imprisonment was permitted by Jesus because it advanced His purposes, and that Jesus was with him to deliver him at the proper time and sustain him in the meantime. As Paul focused on Jesus in this way, God's Spirit sustained him with peace and hope, and empowered him to give God's love to his guards, his visitors, his colleagues—and to the Colossians. Maybe this is one reason why Paul passed this song on to them!

This is why spiritual songs are important to me. I don't particularly enjoy singing Christian songs at meetings, and I find many Christian songs cheesy. But I have an "arsenal" of songs that have solid biblical lyrics and musical arrangement that I enjoy. I use them privately, listening to them as I do yard work, or singing them to myself as I walk or drive. The lyrics help my mind to recall the gospel's content, and the melody helps my heart to appreciate who Jesus is and what He did for me. I can thank God through song when it is difficult to speak to Him in my own words. Sometimes the song recurs throughout the day like a commercial jingle—but instead of irritating me with its nonsense, it helps me to stay focused on the gospel!

Do you have your own "arsenal" of spiritual songs? This can help you to stay focused on Jesus and His grace!

Chapter 4
Colossians 1:25-2:1
3 Keys To Victorious Suffering

Paul often digressed when he wrote his letters. One of his letters (2 Corinthians) has a digression that is over four chapters long! His letter to the Colossians also contains a digression. In the midst of explaining who Jesus is (1:15-20) and what Jesus accomplished through His death (2:10-15), Paul includes a digression about his current hardships. I have bolded the terms that relate to his hardships to make this theme apparent.

> [1.24] I rejoice in my **sufferings** for your sake, and in my flesh I do my share on behalf of His body, which is the church, in filling up what is lacking in Christ's **afflictions**. [25] Of this church I was made a minister... [28] We proclaim Him, admonishing every man and teaching every man with all wisdom, so that we may present every man complete in Christ. [29] For this purpose also I **labor**, **striving** according to His power, which mightily works within me. [2.1] For I want you to know how great a **struggle** I have on your behalf and for those who are at Laodicea, and for all those who have not personally seen my face)...

Why does Paul digress? Not to get their pity, but to alleviate their distress. We know from another letter he wrote to other nearby churches that they were tempted to lose heart because of his sufferings.

Therefore I ask you not to lose heart at my tribulations on your behalf, for they are your glory. (Ephesians 3:13)

These Christians loved Paul, even though many of them had never seen him. They may have simply been deeply sad at the prospect of Paul's imprisonment and possible execution. They may have also been thinking: "If following Jesus leads to this, what's the use?"

Paul assures them in this passage that he has not lost heart because of his hardships, and then explains why he is of good courage in the midst of them. This is what we could call *victorious suffering*. The Bible teaches that we cannot escape suffering in this fallen world, but through Christ we can learn how to suffer victoriously. And in this passage, Paul reveals three keys that enable him (and us!) to suffer victoriously. They aren't the only keys, but they will take us a long way!

KEY #1: Understanding where history is headed

If you want to suffer victoriously, you must have a philosophy of history. This may sound abstract and initially irrelevant, but you have to start here. God hard-wired us to need to know where history is headed in order to have an over-arching meaning for own lives. This knowledge is essential for a life of hope, which motivates us to sacrifice and fortifies us to endure sufferings along the way.

Douglas Hyde was a leader in the British Communist movement in the middle of the 20th century. Later, he realized that Communism was false, and he became a committed Christian. In his book, *Dedication and Leadership*, he laments that Communists were far more willing to suffer and sacrifice for their *false* cause than most Christians are willing to suffer and sacrifice for their *true* cause. Why? Because the Communists really believed that "There is a great battle going on all over the world which, in the final analysis is a struggle for men's hearts and minds and souls... (and that) although we may not see the end of the battle, its outcome will most probably be decided in this period in which we are living."[1] It was the Communists' conviction that history is headed toward a classless worker state, and that they had a key part in this outcome, that strengthened them to sacrifice and suffer to advance this cause.

Paul also holds a perspective about human history that dominates his mind and burns in his heart. He knows where history is headed, and he understands the specific stage of history in which he lives. This is what he describes in 1:24-27.

> [24] Now I rejoice in my sufferings for your sake, and in my flesh I do my share on behalf of His body, which is the church, in filling up what is lacking in Christ's afflictions. [25] Of this church I was made a minister according to the stewardship from God bestowed on me for your benefit, so that I might fully carry out the preaching of the word of God, [26] that is, the mystery which has been hidden from the past ages and generations, but has now been manifested to His saints, [27] to whom God willed to make known what is the riches of the glory of this mystery among the Gentiles, which is Christ in you, the hope of glory.

We can summarize the theological content of Paul's philosophy of history in this way:

- God is moving history toward the kingdom of "Christ." As we saw earlier, "Christ" refers to Jesus, and is His title – God's anointed Ruler who will one day rescue the world from evil and re-establish God's righteous rule over all humanity. Paul calls this future kingdom "the hope of glory" because at the end of the age Jesus will appear in all His majesty, and

---

[1] Douglas Hyde, *Dedication and Leadership* (University of Notre Dame Press, 1966), p. 10.

He will then bestow His majesty on all of His followers (see Col. 3:4).

- During the Old Testament period, God worked through the nation of Israel to advance His plan. God promised that His Messiah would descend from their nation, and He gave Israel's prophets specific predictions about the Messiah that would enable them to recognize Him when He came. These predictions identified the Messiah's family tree, the time of His coming, His birth-place, details of His public ministry, and how He would die as a payment for human sin and then be resurrected. Jesus fulfilled all of these predictions.

- But the Old Testament did not clearly reveal the next stage of God's plan. This stage is what Paul calls "the mystery." A "mystery" refers to something that has been kept secret and only now revealed. The "mystery" to which Paul refers is in that in this stage of history, Jesus personally indwells each person who believes in Him regardless of their ethnicity – "Christ in you (Gentiles)." This new multi-ethnic entity, which Paul calls "His Body, the church," has the privilege of spreading the good news about Jesus to all ethnic groups (see Matthew 28:19). Jesus declared that this mission is the most important work in this period of history because its completion will bring His return to rule (see Matthew 24:14).

This perspective on history absolutely gripped Paul. He felt a deep sense of privilege that God had revealed this mystery to him, because previous generations did not have this knowledge (1:26). This understanding fortified him during his sufferings and motivated him to sacrifice.

When I became a Christian in the 1970's, people in our culture disagreed deeply about where history was headed. Some believed in the Communist perspective described above, while others believed in the American dream of world-wide capitalism. Some believed that a technological utopia awaited us, while others believed that a technological catastrophe was imminent. Some believed that science was about to triumph, while others believed that the near future would usher in "age of Aquarius." But most people believed that history was headed *somewhere*. So new Christians (like me) already had this category, and could perhaps more easily adopt the Bible's perspective on history. Analysts note that this emphasis was a key element of the spiritual fervor of the "Jesus Movement" (as this period was called).

Today, however, we live in a culture that is cynical about any claim to know history's direction. Postmodern thought has not only "deconstructed" false political utopian hopes; it has "deconstructed" all claims that human history has a goal. This postmodern cynicism is part of the philosophical "atmosphere" that we breathe without being aware of it. It erodes any category for living for a cause greater than one's own comfort and enjoyment, and therefore erodes any motivation to suffer and sacrifice. If history isn't going anywhere, why shouldn't I just make my bunker as comfortable as possible?

We would expect most non-Christians to be conformed in their thinking to our age of historical cynicism. But it is a terrible tragedy that most western Christians do not differ in this regard. Lacking solid biblical understanding about God's plan for human history, they also lack deep personal convictions about the importance of His plan. And therefore they lack the motivation to suffer and sacrifice that characterized Paul and the early church. Furthermore, when Christianity is gutted of its philosophy of history, we should not be surprised that non-Christians spurn it!

How can you acquire this foundational understanding that will enable you to suffer victoriously? There are no easy short-cuts; it takes time and work and the illumination of God's Spirit, but God will richly reward your effort. Consider these steps that we can all take:

- *Familiarize yourself with fulfilled biblical prophecy.* Only the God of the Bible predicts His plan for humanity *before* He accomplishes it. Because you live two thousand years after the Bible was written, you can confirm hundreds of specific historical predictions that God has already fulfilled. Take the time to acquaint yourself with God's perfect predictive track-record. It will increase your confidence that He will fulfill the rest of His plan.[2]

- *Read quality books that elaborate on God's future plan for human history.* I say "quality" because there are lots of so-called Christian books on this subject that are pure speculation. Others fail to take seriously God's commitment to fulfill all of His promises to the nation of Israel. But there are many solid and readable books that explain God's plan for the end of this age and His eternal kingdom after Jesus' return.[3]

- *Learn about the history of the Christian missions movement.* Jesus predicted that His followers would take the gospel to every ethnic group during this period of history. The progressive fulfillment of this prediction is stunning, but little-known by most western Christians. There are several

---

[2] See especially Dennis McCallum, *Discovering God* (especially Chapters 3-6), and James Rochford, *Evidence Unseen* (Part 4). See also Robert C. Newman, *Evidence for the Christian Faith* and Kenny Barfield, *The Prophet Motive.*

[3] For the end of this age, see Paul Benware, *Understanding End Times Prophecy,* Mark Hitchcock, *The End,* and James Rochford, *Endless Hope or Hopeless End?* For God's Eternal kingdom, see Randy Alcorn, *Heaven.*

sources that will educate, inform and motivate you to play your part in this awesome plan.[4]

KEY #2: Being given a unique role in God's plan

A mother victoriously suffers the labor pains of delivery because she knows she is playing a unique role in a precious event—the birth of her beloved child. Parents of infant children suffer victoriously through sleep-deprived nights because they know their role is critical to their infants' physical well-being. When we are convinced that what we are doing really matters, we are more willing to sacrifice and suffer.

Viktor Frankl, in his book *Man's Search for Meaning*, makes this same point. As a prisoner in a Nazi concentration camp, he noted that only those prisoners who had a meaning for their own lives endured their terrible sufferings with hope and dignity. Those who lacked this meaning, and who lived only to avoid suffering, soon wilted and died. Frankl went on to develop what he called *logotherapy* ("meaning therapy")—a form of psychotherapy that emphasizes having a meaning for your life that is bigger than temporal comfort and circumstantial happiness.

"People have enough to live *by* but nothing to live *for*; they have the *means* but no *meaning*... One of the central tenets of logotherapy (is) that man's main concern is not to gain pleasure or avoid pain but rather to see a meaning in his life. That is why man is even ready to suffer, on the condition... that his suffering has a meaning... Once an

---

[4] See the course "Perspectives on the World Christian Movement," and the book by the same name. See also The Joshua Project (www.joshuaproject.net) to update the progress on God's plan to reach every ethnic group with the gospel. George Eldon Ladd's "When Will the Kingdom Come?" in *The Gospel of the Kingdom* is a classic call for Christians to view history in light of God's missions purpose.

individual's search for... meaning is successful, it not only renders him happy but also gives him the capability to cope with suffering."[5]

Unfortunately, because Frankl was an agnostic, the best he could do was to urge people to invent their own meaning. But because God exists, and because God can speak to us through his Word and Spirit, we can discover the true meaning of our lives.

Paul suffered victoriously not only because he understood God's plan, but also because he knew God had given him a unique role in His plan. God had chosen Him to be His inspired ambassador to the Gentiles, to explain the gospel to them, and to help them toward spiritual maturity.

> [1,25] Of this church I was made a minister according to the stewardship from God bestowed on me for your benefit, so that I might fully carry out the preaching of the word of God... [28] We proclaim Him, admonishing every man and teaching every man with all wisdom, so that we may present every man complete in Christ. [29] For this purpose also I labor...

Listen to the sense of privilege with which Paul describes his role in another letter:

> To me, the very least of all saints, this grace was given, to preach to the Gentiles the unfathomable riches of Christ, and to bring to light what is the administration of the mystery which for ages has been hidden in God... (Ephesians 3:8-9)

Paul knew that he deserved God's condemnation because he had been a religious bigot who persecuted and killed Jesus' followers. But Jesus not only forgave him; He also gave him the ironic privilege of

---

[5] Viktor E. Frankl, *Man's Search for Meaning* (Washington Square Press, 1985), pp. 135,136,163,165.

leading Gentiles to faith and helping them to mature in their faith. This is why Paul can say he doesn't lose heart, but even rejoices, in spite of his sufferings (1:24). He sees that *his sufferings have meaning*, that they are worthwhile because they advance God's plan to redeem other people. His sufferings are "for your sake," they are "on behalf of His Body," they are "for your benefit," they help to "present (you) complete in Christ." This is what Paul means when he says that he does his part in "filling up that which is lacking in Christ's afflictions" (1:24b). Jesus' suffering on the cross was fully sufficient to pay the penalty for our sins (see Col. 2:10-14), but in order for the world to benefit from what He did, His followers have to spread this news. And in order to spread this news, each of us has to endure some sufferings.

While Paul's specific role in God's plan was unique, God has given each Christian a unique role. This point, which is implicit in Col. 1:24-29, Paul makes explicit in another letter:

> For we are God's workmanship, created in Christ Jesus for good works, which God prepared beforehand so that we would walk in them. (Ephesians 2:10)

"Workmanship" is the Greek word *poiema*, from which we get the word "poem." God is writing His grand Story of redemption, and He wants to write our lives as a unique poem in His Story. Before we were ever born, He prepared significant works in His plan for each of us to accomplish. Before we were ever born, God ordained the specific time and place in which we would serve Him. Before we were ever born, God decided the unique combination of natural talents and spiritual gifts with which He would equip us.

This means that, like Paul, you also can play a unique role in helping other people come to faith in Christ. As Tim Keller says:

"There are hands out there that only you can hold. There are people out there that only you can reach. There are hearts breaking that only you can heal... God made you like a fingerprint, and there are certain people out there that He wants to touch through you, and they're not going to be touched without you. So go..."[6]

This means that, like Paul, you also can also play a unique role in helping other Christians to mature in their faith. (We will explore this further in the next chapter.) Ask God to open your eyes to this amazing truth about His unique calling for your life (see Ephesians 1:18a). When you catch even a glimpse of God's vision for your life, your sufferings and sacrifices will still hurt—but they will not crush you because the meaning of your life outweighs them!

KEY #3: Having access to God's power

If you want to be able to suffer victoriously, you need to understand God's plan, you need to see something of the unique role God has given you—and you need access to God's power. That's what Paul has:

> For this purpose also I labor, striving according to His power, which mightily works within me. (Colossians 1:29)

Paul suffers in his service to help others mature in Christ. The Greek word translated "striving" is *agonizomai*, from which our word "agonize" comes. Serving Christ is sometimes agonizing indeed. But if we serve by the power of God, our sufferings will not crush us. God's power is more than sufficient to enable us to keep going despite our suffering. You may remember that earlier in this letter, Paul promised access to God's power to all Christians for this purpose:

(We can be) strengthened with all power, according to His glorious might, for the attaining of all steadfastness and patience... (Colossians 1:11)

---

[6] Tim Keller in a teaching entitled "Witness."

How do you gain access to the power of God? The Bible has much to say in answer to this question, but we can distill three main answers:

- *Receive Christ as your Savior.* You can't access God's power until the Holy Spirit indwells you. And the Bible says that the Holy Spirit indwells you the moment you believe in the gospel.

In Christ, you also, after listening to the message of truth, the gospel of your salvation—having also believed, you were sealed in Him with the Holy Spirit of promise, who is given as a pledge of our inheritance... (Ephesians 1:13,14)

If you try to live your life by your own power, your sufferings will crush you. But you can make one decision that will change this. You can call out to Jesus in faith and receive Him as your Savior. In the moment you entrust yourself to Him, He will forgive you of all of your sins and send His Spirit to live permanently in your heart. And then you will have access to His power!

- Once you have received Christ, you need to *align yourself with God's purpose.* Why is it that so many true Christians, who are indwelt by God's Spirit, do not experience His power? The Holy Spirit is not a force or a genie that you can use for your own purposes. He is a Person who empowers you to accomplish God's purpose—to draw people to faith in Jesus and to help them to mature in Jesus. Is that your purpose? Have you ever given yourself to Him, to be His instrument to accomplish His purpose (Romans 6:13)? You could do this today, and begin to experience the Spirit's power to make you steadfast in God's service!

- If you are indwelt by God's Spirit and aligned with His purpose, *ask God for the power of His Spirit in each situation.* In Luke 11, Jesus told a parable to illustrate His disciples' need for God's provision in order to serve others.

Then He urged them to keep asking God for this provision.
Then He assured them that God would answer their
requests by giving them whatever provision of the Holy
Spirit they needed in their service.

"If you then, being evil, know how to give good gifts to your
children, how much more will your heavenly Father give the Holy
Spirit to those who ask Him?" (Luke 11:13)[7]

You may be indwelt by the Spirit, and be aligned with God's
purpose—but lack the power of the Holy Spirit simply because you
don't regularly ask Him! How often do you ask? Over the last week,
when you were reaching out to people who don't know Christ, or
when you were trying to help other Christians to mature in Him,
how often did you consciously ask your Father for the power of His
Holy Spirit? Ask this coming week, and see the difference!

In a culture that lacks a category for victorious suffering, God wants
to show through His people that this is possible. Will you take Paul's
lessons to heart so that God can work through you in this way?

---

[7] Jesus is not predicting that His followers will soon receive the Holy Spirit. The continuous
tense of the verbs in 11:9,10 refers to an ongoing asking. The absence of the definite article in
11:13 (literally, "will give Holy Spirit") suggests the ongoing reception of the operations of the
Holy Spirit for ministry, rather than the one-time indwelling of the Holy Spirit. See Oswald
Sanders, *In Pursuit of Maturity* (Lamplighter), pp. 211,212.

Chapter 5
Colossians 1:28,29
Disciple-making

As we saw in the previous chapter, Paul digresses in Colossians 1:24-2:1 to explain his ministry calling and the sufferings he experiences in it. Some aspects of Paul's ministry are unique to him. For example, he is a cross-cultural missionary to first-century Mediterranean Gentiles. But another aspect of his ministry, as we will see, is not unique at all. He describes it this way:

[1:28] We proclaim Him, admonishing every person and teaching every person with all wisdom, so that we may present every person complete in Christ. [29] For this purpose also I labor, striving according to His power, which mightily works within me.

In this chapter, we will take a close look at how these verses answer three questions: What is this ministry? Who is to do it? How should we do it?

What is this ministry?

Some people call this ministry "mentoring." Some call it "developing." I'll call it "disciple-making" since that's what Jesus called it:

> "Go therefore and *make disciples* of all the nations, baptizing them in the name of the Father and the Son and the Holy Spirit, teaching them to observe all that I commanded you..." (Matthew 28:19)

The point is that this ministry is *helping individual Christians toward spiritual maturity.* The goal, Paul says, is to present "every

47

person" complete in Christ. "Complete" is the Greek word *teleios*. It does not connote moral perfection in this context (which none of us attains in this life!), but rather reaching one's intended goal, developing one's potential, accomplishing one's intended purpose. When Paul uses this term with reference to Christians, he usually means becoming spiritually mature.[1] You may remember that Paul gave us a snapshot of spiritual maturity in Colossians 1:10-12 (see Chapter 2).

Notice that Paul uses the phrase "every person" three times in 1:28. Here he is referring not to all humanity, but to all Christians. God wants each and every one of His children to grow to spiritual maturity! Now, you can't mature as God's child until you first become God's child—and you become God's child by personally receiving Christ (John 1:12). But once you become God's child, it is His will for you to grow into a spiritual adult. Just as it is a tragedy when people remain immature in basic human development, it is also a tragedy when Christians remain immature in their spiritual lives. It is a tragedy because God doesn't get the honor He deserves, His children don't enjoy the privileges He gave them, and the watching world does not see that Jesus changes lives. This problem is epidemic in American Christianity, as we will see, and the main reason is simple and avoidable.

According to Paul, spiritual maturity requires the intentional help of other Christians. That's why he speaks of "*presenting* every person mature in Christ." When Christ returns, we are to present to God those Christians whom we have intentionally helped to mature—not

---

[1] See Eph. 4:13 – "...until we all attain to the unity of the faith, and of the knowledge of the Son of God, to a mature (*teleios*) man, to the measure of the stature which belongs to the fullness of Christ."

as trophies that testify to how great we are, but as a crucial part of our service for Him.[2] This implies an answer to the second question...

Who is to do it?

Paul indicates that helping individual Christians toward spiritual maturity is *the privilege and responsibility of each and every Christian.*

In Colossians 1:25-27, Paul uses the singular pronoun "I" to describe the unique aspects of his personal ministry. Then in Colossians 1:28, he switches to the plural pronoun "we" as he describes this ministry, and then switches back to "I" in Colossians 1:29. Why this sudden switch to "we?" Probably because Paul wants to emphasize that he is one of *many* people ("we") who do this ministry. The "we" may refer to Paul's church-planting team, but more likely it refers to all Christians. This seems clear because of the parallel passage later in this letter:

Let the word of Christ richly dwell within you, with all wisdom teaching and admonishing one another... (Colossians 3:16)

Notice the similarity between Colossians 1:28 and Colossians 3:16. The *content* in both verses is the same—"Christ" in 1:28 and "the word of Christ" in Colossians 3:16. Both phrases refer to the gospel, the message of God's grace. The *means of communication* are the same—"admonishing... and teaching every person with all wisdom" in 1:28 and "with all wisdom teaching and admonishing" in 3:16. Presumably, the *goal* is the same – spiritual maturity. But notice that

---

[2] In one sense, it is Christ who matures Christians because it is His Word and His Spirit that transforms us. This is why Paul can say in Col. 1:22 that "(Jesus) has reconciled you ...in order to *present* you before (God) holy and blameless and beyond reproach." But Jesus has decided to work through the cooperative agency of Christians, His Body. So in another sense, Paul can say in Col. 1:28 that "We proclaim Christ ...that we might *present* every (Christian) complete in Christ."

3:16 explicitly calls *all* of the Christians in Colossae to help "one another" toward this goal. Disciple-making is for all Christians![3]

The failure of the American evangelical church to embrace this mandate may be its most serious problem. Researcher George Barna has shown that although the vast majority of American evangelicals pay lip-service to this ministry, hardly any (including pastors) actually do it.[4] This omission contributes massively to our well-documented evangelistic ineffectiveness. Consider two implications of this omission:

- The local church should be like a healthy family, in which all members take responsibility to help other members grow up into maturity. Spiritual parents develop spiritual children, and spiritual siblings develop one another—and the result is a growing cadre of solid Christian workers.

  When churches do not have this disciple-making ethos, they become more like perpetual day-care centers in which a few exhausted professionals mass-babysit people who remain in spiritual infancy. This situation, which we lament as dysfunctional in our own families, has sadly become the norm in many American churches. Many pastors lament that they have to do all of the spiritual work in their churches—yet they fail to teach and model and facilitate disciple-making as the priority ministry for their people.

---

[3] Jesus' command to "make disciples" (Matt. 28:18-20) also applies to all Christians, since He called His followers to do this globally ("all nations") throughout the rest of this age until He returns ("to the end of the age").

[4] "(Evangelical) churches have done a good job of promoting the importance of spiritual maturity, but they have mostly failed to provide an environment in which spiritual growth is a lifestyle ...This is partially attributable to our focus on providing programs rather than relationships that support growth.... Our interviews with churches indicate that few churches are intentionally raising up mentors and strategically matching them with congregants." George Barna, *Growing True Disciples* (Waterbrook Press, 2001), p. 55.

- When a local church has an organic network of these relationships, the result is a real, loving community that attracts lost people to Jesus. Jesus loved His disciples toward spiritual maturity, and He told them that loving one another in this way would provide a compelling demonstration to non-Christians that He is alive and accessible.

"A new commandment I give to you, that you love one another, even as I have loved you, that you also love one another. By this all men will know that you are My disciples, if you have love for one another." (John 13:34-35)

When these discipling relationships are lacking, there is no authentic Christian community. Instead, most members live in isolation, spiritually weak and therefore vulnerable to various temptations. We should not be surprised that churches like this don't attract many lost people to Christ. No wonder Satan wants to convince Christians that disciple-making is optional! No wonder he works so hard to convince pastors that "no one would be willing to do this."

If you are not convinced in your heart that disciple-making is Jesus' will for you and for all of your Christian friends, prayerfully ponder the passages cited above. Let God speak to you through them until you can say like Paul: "For this purpose I labor!"

How should we do it?

If you are convinced that disciple-making is every Christian's responsibility, you will want to know how to carry out this ministry. Before we consider Paul's answers to this question, we need to understand an important qualification: While all Christians should practice a disciple-making ministry, this does not mean that all Christians must practice it in exactly the same way. There is lots of

room for personal diversity within this uniform call. Consider the
following:

- Some of us may primarily disciple much younger Christians,
  while some may primarily disciple spiritual peers.
  Discipleship is not one-sided; younger, growing Christians
  often help older Christians toward maturity! Paul's
  exhortation in Colossians 3:16 that we disciple "one
  another" allows for this kind of diversity.

- Some of us will exclusively disciple people within our own
  small groups, while some of us will also disciple others
  beyond our small groups. Disciple-making is most effective
  with people who are in the same small group because they
  can have much more contact with one another in this
  context. Faithful disciple-makers often discover that God
  eventually expands their impact by leading people outside
  their small groups to them for discipleship.

- Some of us may disciple as our primary ministry, while some
  of us may disciple along with many other ministries. This is
  not to say that disciple-making excuses us from other
  biblically-mandated ministries, such as evangelism,
  intercessory prayer, and financial stewardship. In the same
  way, our differing spiritual gifts do not excuse us from
  being involved in disciple-making.

- Some of us, because of opportunity, spiritual gifting,
  spiritual maturity, or stage of life, have the capacity to
  disciple many people, while some of us will have the
  capacity to disciple only one or two people.

- Some of us may prefer to disciple others one-on-one, while
  some of us find that we can also disciple in a small group
  setting. "Small group" here means "small"—three or at most
  four people. Larger small groups are effective for

supplementing these discipleship relationships, but they cannot *replace* them, as they cannot have the kind of personal interaction described below.

Within this diversity, God calls each of us to embrace disciple-making, to ask Him to show us who to disciple, and to take initiative to actually do it. Paul provides several important guidelines on how to disciple in this passage.

First, notice that disciple-making requires focusing together on God's Word—the Bible. "We proclaim Christ" in Colossians 1:28 means: "We communicate the message about Jesus to one another." You can see this same emphasis in Colossians 3:16—"Let the word of Christ richly dwell within you" emphasizes that biblical truth should saturate these relationships. This should not surprise us, since many biblical passages teach that spiritual maturity requires regular intake of God's Word.

How should we communicate God's Word to one another? We should use it to "admonish and teach" one another. "Teach" is *didasko*, which means to explain or to instruct. We help one another to become familiar with the Bible and to understand its perspective on every major area of life. But our goal is not just familiarity with biblical truth. "Admonish" is *neutheteo*, which means to personally apply God's Word to one another's life-situations by way of counsel, warning, correction, or exhortation. "With all wisdom" doesn't mean "with all the wisdom in the universe;" it means "with all the wisdom we have." Wisdom in the Bible is not about abstract or theoretical biblical knowledge; it is skill in applying God's Word in everyday life.

You don't have to be a biblical expert to do this! You can simply take turns reading aloud a biblical book a paragraph at a time and discussing it. Or you can do the same thing with a quality Christian book. This leads us in a natural way to discuss the practical application of biblical truth to our lives. When you meet weekly for a couple of hours for this purpose, and when such meetings accompany serving together in the same small group or ministry, the result is a Christ-centered friendship that leads to increasing spiritual maturity in both people's lives.[5]

Another key part of this long-term effort is praying for one another. Paul makes this point later in this letter.

Epaphras... sends you his greetings, always laboring earnestly for you in his prayers, that you may stand mature and fully assured in all the will of God. (Colossians 4:12)

Epaphras is helping the Colossian Christians to mature by "laboring earnestly" (*agonizomai*) in his prayers for them. Praying *for* one another, which includes praying *with* one another, is a key part of helping each other toward maturity. We unleash God's maturing power into one another's lives as we pray for insight into God's Word, for exposure of satanic lies, for encouragement during adversity, for motivation and wisdom to love the people in our lives, etc.

Spiritual maturity will not happen quickly! It takes sustained commitment. This is why Paul says: "For this purpose I labor, striving..." "Labor" is *kopaio*, which described the day-after-day, all-day work that first-century farmers performed. "Striving" is *agonizomai* (from which we get "agonize," which described the endurance of marathon runners. By using both of these verbs, Paul is emphasizing that disciple-making involves intensive effort over a long period of time. Because spiritual maturity takes a long time, we make a commitment to meet regularly to teach, admonish and pray

---

[5] "Regular personal appointments will help us minister to personal needs and help point to ways of dealing with issues (we) face in life ...(and) ensure that we are taught the basics of Christianity and begin to feel at home with the Bible." Ajith Fernando, *The Call to Joy and Pain* (Crossway, 2007), p. 163.

for one another over the long haul—usually for years, not just for weeks or months. In my experience, much disciple-making is ineffective simply because the people involved don't stick at it.

America is a "quick fix" culture. But real spiritual maturity is never a quick fix. It is in committed Christian friendships built around God's Word and prayer that God gradually transforms us to be more like Christ. This is neither fancy nor dramatic—and definitely not quick—but it is effective like nothing else!

About now you might be thinking: "Where will I get the energy and stamina to do this?" That's precisely why Paul ends the way he does in Colossians 1:29: "...I labor, striving according to His power which mightily works within me." "Power" and "works" are *energeia*, from which we get our words "energy" and "energize." "Mightily" is *dunamis*, from which we get our words "dynamic" and "dynamite."

God's Holy Spirit, who dwells within each of God's children, constantly imparts to us the power to steadfastly and patiently help one another along the long road toward spiritual maturity![6] He also imparts wisdom to apply biblical truth to this end. Why do some Christians get "burned out" in disciple-making, while others thrive in it year after year? One key reason is that the latter have learned to regularly ask the Holy Spirit to empower them and give them wisdom for this work. Those who align their lives to make disciples, and who regularly ask the Holy Spirit to empower them for this purpose, receive divine resources for their work!

I have experienced much joy in over forty years of Christian ministry—joy from seeing people come to faith in Christ, joy from seeing new churches spring up and prosper, and joy from seeing the gospel spread in other parts of the world. But I would have to agree with John in one of his letters: "I have no greater joy than this, to see

---

[6] Notice how Paul uses these same words in Colossians 1:11 to describe how God enables us to attain to steadfastness and patience the very qualities we need in disciple-making!

my children walking in the truth" (3 John 1:4). My greatest joy has come from being involved in these disciple-making relationships. True, these relationships involve difficulty, and some end badly. When this happens, Satan will tell us that it is not worth the effort and heartache. But protecting our hearts from disappointment will never accomplish God's will for our lives. Besides, these Christ-centered friendships also make possible a quality of Christian fellowship that is uniquely enjoyable. And they result in much fruit that glorifies God, which Jesus promised would make us full with His joy (John 15:8-11). So disciple-making and a life of joy go together!

Chapter 6
Colossians 2:1-8
Key Ingredients of Spiritual Maturity

^{2.1} For I want you to know how great a struggle I have on your behalf and for those who are at Laodicea, and for all those who have not personally seen my face, ² that their hearts may be encouraged, having been knit together in love, and attaining to all the wealth that comes from the full assurance of understanding, resulting in a true knowledge of God's mystery, that is, Christ Himself, ³ in whom are hidden all the treasures of wisdom and knowledge. ⁴ I say this so that no one will delude you with persuasive argument. ⁵ For even though I am absent in body, nevertheless I am with you in spirit, rejoicing to see your good discipline and the stability of your faith in Christ. ⁶ Therefore as you have received Christ Jesus the Lord, so walk in Him, ⁷ having been firmly rooted and now being built up in Him and established in your faith, just as you were instructed, and overflowing with gratitude. ⁸ See to it that no one takes you captive through philosophy and empty deception, according to the tradition of men, according to the elementary principles of the world, rather than according to Christ. (Colossians 2:1-8)

In the previous chapter, we saw that Paul calls all Christians to help one another toward spiritual maturity. He says in 1:29 that this work involves intensive "striving"—*agonizomai*, from which we get our word "agonize." Paul uses this word again 2:1 as he describes his "struggle" to help the Colossian church and other nearby churches toward spiritual maturity.

In 2:2-7, Paul speaks of several key ingredients of Christian spiritual maturity. An ingredient isn't the finished product; it is a component that is essential in order to get the finished product. The Colossian Christians already had some of these ingredients, so Paul rejoices in this fact. They lacked other ingredients, so he urges them to give attention to these. We need to know what these ingredients are, because if we lack them, we will not be able to mature nor will we be able to help others to mature. I see four key ingredients here; let's cover them in a different order.

Ingredient #1: Receive Christ

[6] Therefore as you have received Christ Jesus the Lord, so walk in Him...

Spiritual maturity requires receiving Christ Jesus as Lord. Just as you can't mature physically until you are born physically, you can't mature spiritually until you are born spiritually. And the only way you get born spiritually is by receiving Christ Jesus as Lord.

To "receive *Christ Jesus the Lord*" involves adopting the right view of Jesus. He isn't one of many ways to God, or merely a good moral example, or a master teacher/spiritual guru. He is the "Christ"— God's chosen King, predicted by the Old Testament prophets that His death paid for our sins, and that He will return to establish God's rule over all humanity. He is the "Lord"—the one and only rightful Ruler of your life.

To "*receive* Christ Jesus the Lord" also means that you make a conscious decision to personally receive Jesus. "Receive" (*proslambano*) means "to join to oneself." When Joseph "took" (same word) Mary as his wife, he personally chose to be joined with her for life. Likewise, receiving Christ is more than intellectually assenting that He is the Christ. It means that you take the living Jesus as your Messiah, and that you welcome Him into your heart and life (Revelation 3:20). It is when you receive Christ that His Spirit comes to live in your heart to give you the desire and ability to mature. Have you "received Christ Jesus the Lord?"

Ingredient #2: Receive ongoing instruction about Christ

[6] Therefore as you have received Christ Jesus the Lord, so walk in Him, [7] having been firmly rooted and now being built up in Him and established in your faith, just as you were instructed, and overflowing with gratitude.

Just as we received Christ by faith, we are to choose to "walk in Him." In both cases, we make a choice to entrust ourselves to Christ. The verb tenses here inform us that while receiving Christ is a one-time decision ("just as you received Christ"), walking in Him is an ongoing decision ("so keep walking in Him"). Walking physically is not dramatic or sporadic; it is one foot in front of another over a long period of time. Likewise, walking in Christ is a daily decision to actively entrust ourselves to Him.

Walking in Him requires receiving ongoing instruction in the New Testament message about Jesus. That's why Paul says "just as you were *instructed*." Just as a baby will not develop properly without an ongoing regimen of nutrition, so we will not develop spiritually without an ongoing regimen of quality biblical instruction. Many American Christians remain in spiritual immaturity simply because they are malnourished in this sense! We can get some of this instruction through quality Christian books and recorded teachings, but we also need frequent in-person Bible teaching and discussion. The Christians in Jerusalem, for instance, did not just go to a Bible study once a week—they "continuously devoted" themselves to this kind of instruction (Acts 2:42).

Paul describes two different stages of this crucial ingredient. First we
need to be "rooted." This is an *agricultural* word (*rizoo*), from which
we get "rhizome." New plants need to develop a good root system in
order to grow to maturity. New Christians also need to develop a
good root system, and you do this by getting solid instruction on the
basics of what Jesus did for you on the cross. Only when you are
thus rooted will you have a stable basis for development. Paul
explains these "basics" in Colossians 2:10-15, and we will explore
his instruction in the next chapter.

Then we need to be "built up and established." These are both
architectural terms which mean to build the structure on the
foundation that has already been laid. Whereas "being rooted" is in
the perfect tense (something completed in the past), "built up and
established" are in the present (ongoing) tense. In other words, we
need to keep adding to our understanding of the gospel for the rest
of our lives. What Jesus has given us is so vast that we will never
reach a complete comprehension of it.[1] A healthy Christian life is
like the scene in the movie "National Treasure" when Nicolas Cage
and his friends discover the national treasure. Their initial glimpse
by torch-light elicits a "Wow"—but as additional light reveals a vast
room filled with innumerable treasures, they keep saying "Wow!"
Likewise, in a maturing Christian life, the Holy Spirit keeps showing
us from scripture more of what Christ has done for us and how
much God loves us. And we keep getting more impressed and
thankful for this—"overflowing with gratitude." Paul will explain
this process more in Colossians 3:1-4, and we will explore his
instruction in a later chapter.

Unfortunately, many Christians do not continue to be built up and
established. They settle for being rooted only. They think they "get it"

---

[1] In Ephesians 3:8, Paul speaks of this as "the unfathomable riches of Christ." In
Ephesians 3:18,19, he prays for Christians to comprehend more deeply the scope of Christ's
love, even though it surpasses our full comprehension.

when they have only scratched the surface. They lose their thankfulness and joy, and even cop an attitude of bored entitlement. As a result, they do not gain strength to keep maturing, and they become vulnerable to all kinds of spiritual dysfunctions.

Ingredient #3: Develop resistance to spiritual deception

> [4] I say this so that no one will delude you with persuasive argument... [8] See to it that no one takes you captive through philosophy and empty deception, according to the tradition of men, according to the elementary principles of the world, rather than according to Christ.

In order to mature, each of us must also develop resistance to spiritual deception. We do not live in a spiritually positive or even neutral environment. There are demonic spirits who want to "take us captive" so that even as Christians we serve their ends rather than God's. Their normal mode of attack is "delusion"—deception through people who are very persuasive!

The Colossians faced sophisticated *spiritual* deception. Eloquent teachers were re-inventing Jesus in ways that denied His deity and minimized the importance of His death. They also redefined spiritual maturity and advocated erroneous spiritual practices to attain it. This same kind of religious deception is operative today, and in the next two chapters we will learn how to avoid this kind of capture.

But there are other forms of *secular* deception that can sabotage your spiritual maturity. Peers, authority figures, and media voices can be unwittingly used by demons to deceive you into looking for comfort and joy from substance abuse. Or to look for security from romantic relationships that compromise God's moral will. Or to look for significance from money and career advancement.

While our society disapproves of some of these deceptions (like substance abuse), it is neutral toward others (like many forms of sexual immorality) and actually approves of others (like careerism). Over the years, I have seen hundreds of Christians fail to mature because they fell prey to these forms of deception. It is heart-breaking and very sobering. I look at the Christians around me and wonder: "Who will be taken out by spiritual deception over the next few years?"

Then I look at myself and wonder: "Why have I not been taken out by deception? Where am I most vulnerable?" Do you ever ask yourself these questions? If not, is it because you have an unfounded confidence that you are spiritually safe? Paul warns us: "Do you think you stand firm? Take heed lest you fall" (1 Corinthians 10:12).

How can we cultivate resistance to spiritual deception?

- The best defense is a good offense! Keep growing in your knowledge of the gospel (as described above), and you will be both more sensitized to deception and less attracted to it.

- Practice critical thinking. Listen for the beliefs and values people communicate at work and school, through the media, and in daily conversations. Consciously compare what you hear and read to what the Bible says. Practice this, and over time you will train your senses to detect deception.

  For everyone who partakes only of milk is not accustomed to the word of righteousness, for he is an infant. But solid food is for the mature, who because of practice have their senses trained to discern good and evil. (Hebrews 5:13,14)

- Perhaps the most important way to protect yourself against deception is the fourth ingredient that Paul describes in this passage...

Ingredient #4: Live "in formation" with other Christians

> [5] For even though I am absent in body, nevertheless I am with you in spirit, rejoicing to see your good discipline and the stability of your faith in Christ.

Paul rejoices because the Colossian Christians already have this ingredient in place. Unfortunately, our English translations don't adequately convey what it is. Both phrases ("good discipline" and "stability") have a military background. "Good discipline" (*taxis*) means "in right order or in formation."[2] "The stability of your faith" (*stereoma*) means "a solid military front."[3] Paul describes the Colossian church as like a Roman maniple (see below).

This highly disciplined battle formation enabled the soldiers to form a solid wall that warded off numerous and powerful enemies.

Likewise, the Colossian church was not a rabble of isolated, autonomous individuals. Rather, they lived "in formation" with one another.[4] They were an organized network of caring relationships (2:2 "knitted together in love"), relationships that were close enough that they could

---

[2] Strong, J. (2001). *Enhanced Strong's Lexicon.* Bellingham, WA.: Logos Bible Software.

[3] Strong, J. (2001). *Enhanced Strong's Lexicon.* Bellingham, WA.: Logos Bible Software.

[4] This "maniple" formation also informs Paul's description of "putting on the full armor of God" in Eph. 6:10-17. While western Christians presume Paul is speaking primarily about individual spiritual warfare, he in fact presumes that Christians should fight together in this way.

watch one another's backs. In other words, they were organized the way we learned in the previous chapter—a network of Christ-centered friendships that met regularly to prayerfully read and discuss biblical truth.

Are you "in formation," or are you an isolated candidate for deception? With whom do you regularly meet for this purpose? Are you open with them about your current struggles, fears, and doubts? Are you responsive when they express concern for your spiritual welfare? Are you watching their backs in the same way? This is living "in formation." This is how spiritual deception gets nipped in the bud, and this is how we grow toward maturity!

Putting it together

Paul did not suggest that any of these ingredients was optional. Rather, the New Testament teaches that each of these ingredients is necessary for spiritual maturity. Being strong in one ingredient cannot make up for weakness or omission of another ingredient. I know many Christians who are very knowledgeable in the Bible, for example, but who do not live "in formation." As a result, they live stunted spiritual lives and often fall prey to crippling deception. Which ingredient do you most lack? Strengthen that one, without neglecting the rest. And help your Christian friends to do this also!

Chapter 7
Colossians 2:8-15
The Cross: God's Radical Provision

[2.8] See to it that no one takes you captive through philosophy and empty deception, according to the tradition of men, according to the elementary principles of the world, rather than according to Christ. [9] For in Him all the fullness of Deity dwells in bodily form, [10] and in Him you have been made complete...

The false teachers in Colossae were evidently teaching that there was a spiritual "fullness" (*pleroma*) that the Christians lacked. In order to obtain this fullness, they needed to "graduate" beyond Jesus (whom the false teachers viewed as a lesser spirit) into devotion to other spiritual rulers and other spiritual practices. Paul warns them against these false teachers, and gives very different counsel:

- "You don't need to 'graduate' beyond Jesus, because Jesus is the fullness (*pleroma*) of deity in bodily form, and He is far above all other spiritual rulers. To 'graduate' beyond Jesus is actually a trap that will hurt you spiritually."

- "You don't need other spiritual practices because you are already complete (*pleroo*) in Christ."[1] Since Jesus is like a mine full of spiritual treasures (2.3), spiritual maturity isn't moving on to a better mine (there isn't one); it is becoming more familiar with the treasures you already have in Jesus

---

[1] While "complete" in 1.28 is *teleios*, and means "mature, "complete" in " 2.10 is *pleroo* and means "fully resourced" – having received through Jesus all the resources needed to mature.

and mining them so that you can enrich your life and
others' lives.

Specifically, Jesus' death on the cross provides us these resources.
The cross is God's radical provision for our spiritual lives. "Radical"
derives from the word *radix*, which means "root." We have many
problems in our lives, but some are symptomatic problems, while
others are root problems. In Colossians 2:11b–15, Paul reveals three
of our root problems, and how the cross of Christ provides the
solution to these problems. Let's take a look at each of them, starting
with the one easiest to understand.

The cross has canceled your "certificate of debt"

[13] When you were dead in your transgressions and the
uncircumcision of your flesh, He made you alive together with Him,
having forgiven us all our transgressions, [14] having canceled out the
certificate of debt consisting of decrees against us, which was hostile
to us; and He has taken it out of the way, having nailed it to the
cross.

The first provision we receive is God's *cancellation of our "certificate
of debt."* Certificates of debt were legal statements of either personal
financial debt or criminal guilt. You get a certificate of debt when
you receive a traffic ticket or a guilty verdict for a felony. It states
your violation and the penalty for it.

Paul says we all have a certificate of debt with God, and this is one of
our root problems. Every time we violate His perfect moral character
in thought, word or deed, we accumulate true moral guilt before a
righteous God. This guilt is "hostile" to us because it brings us under
God's judgment, since the wages of sin is death (Romans 6:23).

Our culture has a huge blind-spot here. We recognize the reality
and destructive power of guilt, but we tend to view guilt only in
psychological (guilt feelings) or sociological (criminal acts) terms.

Although these kinds of guilt are real, the Bible says that the most serious kind of guilt is theological. We are convicted felons before *God.* Therefore, any real solution to our guilt must deal with *His* certificate of debt.

Here we find a similarity and dissimilarity between Christianity and many of the other religions of the world. They are similar in that they acknowledge the reality of true moral guilt before God. But they are dissimilar in their solution to this problem. Most other religions say. "You must pay your own debt." That's why there is no assurance of God's acceptance in any of them. But Christianity says, "God has already paid your debt through Jesus' death on the cross."

Jesus had a Roman certificate of debt nailed to His cross. It was the Roman charge of sedition – that He claimed to be King of the Jews. But He was innocent of this crime since He was the rightful King. In fact, He was innocent of *all* sin before God; He was the only Person without a divine certificate of debt! Instead, God took all our certificates of debt and "nailed them to the cross." In other words, He applied all of our guilt to Jesus and judged Him in our place.

When a criminal had served his punishment, the authorities wrote the word *tetelestai* ("paid in full") across his certificate,[2] which he could then produce to prove he was no longer punishable for that crime. Just before Jesus died, He cried out "It is finished!" (Jn. 19.30). This is the same word *tetelestai.* Jesus was saying. "I have now paid your debt in full through My death!" That's why Paul says that through the cross God "has forgiven all your transgressions," "has canceled out" your certificate of debt, and "has taken it out of the way."

How can you apply this radical provision? The first step is to simply to *receive Jesus' full payment for your sins.* Imagine being hopelessly

---

[2] Moulton and Milligan, *Vocabulary of the Greek New Testament* (Eerdmans, 1974), p. 630.

in debt with no bankruptcy provision. Then imagine that a
benefactor cuts you a check that covers your entire debt. The issue is
no longer your debt; it is your willingness to endorse the check and
deposit it in your account. In the same way, it is no longer your sins,
but your willingness to receive Jesus' gift of forgiveness that is the
crucial issue. Will you call out to God, acknowledge your certificate
of debt to Him – and ask Him to cancel it through Jesus' death? The
moment you do this, God wipes out your entire sin-debt forever, and
permanently accepts you as if you had never sinned against Him!

Once you have received God's complete forgiveness, you will need to
appropriate it for subsequent sins. Instead of punishing yourself or
assuming that God has distanced Himself from you, draw near to
Him and agree with Him – that what you have done is wrong, and
that He has already forgiven you for it. Thank Him for this, and then
resume relating to Him and letting Him work through you. This is
what the author of Hebrews reminds us:

How much more, then, will the blood of Christ, who through the
eternal Spirit offered himself unblemished to God, cleanse our
consciences from acts that lead to death, so that we may serve the
living God! (Hebrews 9:14 NIV)

The cross has given you a spiritual "circumcision"

> 2:11...and in Him you were also circumcised with a
> circumcision made without hands, in the removal of the
> body of the flesh by the circumcision of Christ; 12 having
> been buried with Him in baptism, in which you were also
> raised up with Him through faith in the working of God,
> who raised Him from the dead.

Through the cross of Christ, God has made another radical provision
for another root problem – He has *given you a spiritual*

circumcision. The false teachers were apparently urging the
Colossian Christians to undergo physical circumcision as a step
toward spiritual enlightenment. Paul says this is unnecessary
because they have already been spiritually circumcised by Jesus.
What does this mean?

Circumcision was an Old Testament ritual which God prescribed for
male Israelites for several reasons. In Deuteronomy, God told them
that circumcision was a symbol of their need for radical spiritual
surgery – to be delivered from their rebellious sinful nature.

> "So circumcise your heart, and stiffen your neck no longer."
> (Deuteronomy 10:16)

Not only do our sins violate God's standard and accumulate a
certificate of debt; we are also slaves to sin – in bondage to a sinful
nature.[3] We commit sins because we are slaves to sin. God diagnosed
this as a heart problem that requires heart surgery.

This is a problem with which most of us do not come to grips until
after we receive God's forgiveness through faith in Christ. We now
have a new nature that wants to follow God's will, but we discover
that there is something within us that is still deeply self-centered
and aversive to God. We discover that even though we have been
delivered some obvious destructive behaviors, the roots of those
behaviors are as strong as ever. For example, I was intensely
competitive before I received Christ. I was often overtly hostile to
athletic or academic competitors, scorning or cursing them
depending on whether I won or lost. My conversion substantially
eliminated these competitive behaviors, but it didn't eliminate my
competitive heart. Sadly, I noticed that I viewed Christian peers as
rivals in spiritual growth and ministry. I treated them politely, but
inwardly I hated their success and rejoiced at their failures. What is

---

[3] "The body of the flesh" in 2:11 refers to our sinful natures rather than to our physical bodies.

this? This is slavery to my sin nature – something deeper than guilt from my sinful deeds. As Richard Lovelace says:

"In its biblical definition, sin cannot be limited to isolated instances or patterns of wrongdoing; it is something much more akin to the psychological term *complex*: an organic network of compulsive attitudes, beliefs, and behavior deeply rooted in alienation from God... Sinful thoughts, words and deeds flow forth from this darkened heart automatically and compulsively, as water from a polluted fountain." [4]

Unless we understand and apply God's radical solution to this problem, we will fall into one of two errors. The first error is to focus on external rule-keeping – either external prohibitions (e.g., "Don't drink alcohol") or external commands (e.g., "Attend church every Sunday"). This error leads to self-righteousness when you keep the rules, or to hiding when you don't keep them. The second error is to be honest but fatalistic about your sinful nature. You admit that you are pridefully competitive, but conclude "That's just the way I am; no change is possible."

God knew we couldn't solve this problem, so He predicted that His Messiah would provide the solution when He came.

"Moreover the Lord your God will circumcise your heart and the heart of your descendants, to love the Lord your God with all your heart and with all your soul, so that you may live." (Deuteronomy 30:6)

In Colossians 2, Paul says that through Jesus' death on the cross, God has fulfilled His promise to supply this radical surgery. Not only did His death pay for the guilt of our sins; it also removed the authority of our sin-natures so that we can experience growing freedom from

---

[4] Richard Lovelace, *Dynamics of Spiritual Life* (InterVarsity Press, 1979), p. 89.

sin's control.[5] So just as the cross of Christ is the key to dealing with your guilt before God, it is also the key to deep-seated, lasting moral change in your life!

We're going to take a closer look at how to apply this truth to our lives when we get to Colossians 3. But if you have received Christ, this provision means that you should reject the lie that you are doomed to live in slavery to sin in any area of your life. Even though your past experience and feelings may tell you that you're a slave to some sinful habit, choose to affirm with God that He has broken its authority. This is the necessary posture of faith that unleashes His guidance and power to liberate you in His way and timing.

The cross has disarmed the demonic forces that oppose you

[10] He is the head over all rule and authority... [15] When He had disarmed the rulers and authorities, He made a public display of them, having triumphed over them through Him.

The third radical provision God has made through the cross of Christ involves our relationship with supernatural evil – *it has disarmed the demonic forces that oppose you.* These "rulers and authorities" are demonic spirits, which Paul elsewhere calls "the spiritual forces of wickedness in the heavenly places" (Ephesians 6:12). The Bible declares that these evil spirits exist and exert a destructive influence on fallen humanity, ranging from overt control (see for example Mark 5:1-15) to insidious distraction from your need for Christ through the selfish lust and pride that animates Satan's world-system (see 1 John 2:15-17; 5:19). If you receive

---

[5] "Removal" in Colossians 2:11 ("the removal of the body of the flesh") is *apekdusis,* which can also mean "disarm" (see Colossians 2:15). Since Paul teaches that Christians still have a sin-nature (see Romans 7:17,20), this spiritual circumcision involves removing our sin-natures' *authority* rather than removing it altogether. The total removal of our sin-natures will not happen until we receive new bodies when Jesus returns (see Romans 7:24; 8:23).

Christ and follow Him, you will run into the reality of these demonic forces before long. They will not only *tempt* you to disobey God's will, and *accuse* you of being rejected by God, and *cast doubt* on God's truth; they will also *threaten you with disaster* if you keep following Christ and *oppress* you in ways that are sometimes sickening.

What is God's provision for this root problem? You guessed it—Jesus' death on the cross! Jesus is greater in authority and power than any demonic ruler (2:10b). And since sin brought us under their dominion, Jesus' death for our sins also breaks their authority over those who belong to Him by transferring us into His kingdom. Paul stated this earlier in Colossians 1:

For He rescued us from the domain of darkness, and transferred us to the kingdom of His beloved Son, in whom we have redemption, the forgiveness of sins. (Colossians 1:13,14)

Demonic rulers still exist and can still attack you, and though they can never take away your salvation, they can mess up your life if you listen to their lies and obey them. But if you have received Christ, they have been "disarmed"—they have no authority to rule you or to prevent you from accomplishing God's will for your life.

How can we apply this radical solution? There are several ways, but consider these:

- *Renounce all involvement with other spirits.* Since Paul says that God has "made a public display" of these spiritual rulers and "triumphed over them," they are obviously hostile to God and His purposes. This means that those who belong to Christ should not worship them or consort with them for protection or power. No matter how well-intentioned, involvement with these spirits can unleash their destructive power into our lives. This is why the Bible forbids all such practices (Deuteronomy 18:9-14), and why

early Christians confessed and renounced them
(Acts 19:18,19). If you are seeking spiritual protection or
power through spirit guides, mediums, astrology, or other
similar practices, you should terminate these practices
immediately. Jesus is greater than they are, and He has
proven His love for you by dying for your sins. He is the
only One you need for your spiritual life. If you have been
involved in such practices in the past, ask another Christian
to pray with you as you renounce this involvement and
turn from it to follow Jesus only.

- *Present yourself to God as a servant of His kingdom.* The
  Bible teaches that, whether we know it or not, we must
  serve someone—either sin (and its author, Satan) or
  righteousness (and its author, God). It also teaches that we
  come under the influence of the one we serve
  (Romans 6:16-18). So liberation from demonic influence
  comes only to those who present themselves to God as His
  servants. Such a commitment is not a vow to be perfect. It is
  simply saying to the Lord: "I am Your child now through
  faith in Christ, and I want to serve You and advance Your
  purposes. Here is my life; use me as You will." This
  presentation places you under God's authority and
  unleashes His power to guide and protect you.

- *Call out to Jesus when you are terrified by evil spirits.* If you
  give yourself to God to serve Him, don't be surprised if you
  experience some demonic attack. Why should they attack
  you when you are not serving God? You pose no threat to
  them in that state, and they typically "let sleeping dogs lie."
  But those who move forward with God will encounter their
  opposition in ways that can be terrifying. Through grisly
  nightmares, or oppressive gloom, or threats to ruin your life
  or destroy your family, or even demonic visitations, they

seek to intimidate you from serving God. When you experience these attacks, remember that Jesus is with You and that He is stronger than any evil spirit. Call out to Him by name and ask Him to help you. Remind them that you belong to Jesus. The evil spirits fear Him because they know He has defeated them. Jesus may send them away immediately and dramatically. Or He may call on you to press forward through their attacks for a time before He commands them to be gone. Leave these details to Him. Just cling to Him and move forward, and He will deliver you. Jesus is so powerful that He even uses demonic attacks to strengthen your faith (Luke 22:31,32)!

God has fully resourced us through the cross of Christ. We have everything we need to mature in Him. Our part is to focus on these resources, grow in our understanding and appreciation of them, and learn how they apply to the key areas of our lives. Paul will tell us how to do this in Colossians 3 and 4 – but first he warns us against religious practices that are hazardous to our spiritual health.

Chapter 8
Colossians 2:16-23
Religious Practices that Are Hazardous to Your Spiritual Health!

We have learned that the false teachers in Colossae rejected both Jesus' deity and what He accomplished through His death. They also advocated certain religious practices as necessary for spiritual maturity. But Paul warns that these practices are hazardous to their spiritual health because such practices will side-track them from spiritual maturity.

Since these practices originate from human speculation, it should not surprise us that they are central to other world religions. But what is stunning and tragic is that they have been common in most of Christendom for the past 2000 years! It is as though most of the church has never read this passage (or the many other passages like it). If you want to mature spiritually, you must be able to identify these religious practices, resist those who advocate them, and (if needed) root them out of your own life. Paul's tone in this passage is therefore negative—but out of loyalty to Jesus and love for people, not out of mean-spiritedness or superiority.

Ritualism

> 2.16 Therefore no one is to act as your judge in regard to food or drink or in respect to a festival or a new moon or a Sabbath day...

Paul is referring to the rituals prescribed by God in the Old
Testament. The dietary laws and the various holy days of the Jewish
calendar were part of the ritualistic system God prescribed for Israel.
By ritualism, I mean *relating to God primarily through prescribed
rituals.* The Colossian Christians had not been practicing these
rituals. But when the false teachers began judging them as
unspiritual for their non-practice, they evidently began to waver.

Ritualism is a key component of virtually all major world religions
except for biblical Christianity. Sacred places and times, sacrifices,
dietary laws, priests, scripted prayers—this is the stuff of religious
activity. Of course, many "Christian" denominations are extremely
ritualistic, complete with liturgical worship services, religious
calendars that include dietary restrictions during certain periods,
and sacred buildings. Ritualism dominates the landscape of
Christendom so much that when I tell people that biblical
Christianity is not ritualistic, they usually look at me like I must be
crazy. Yet this is exactly what Paul is saying in Colossians 2:16!

Why does Paul warn us against ritualism? The answer is found in
the next verse.

> [2:17] (These things) are a mere shadow of what is to come; but
> the substance belongs to Christ.

Ritualism is profoundly out of synch with what God is doing because
it focuses on the "shadows" instead of the "substance" or "reality." The
Old Testament rituals were "shadows" of Christ. Its ritual system was
a divinely inspired multi-media presentation which communicated
the main elements of God's plan of salvation.

- The Tabernacle pictured God's desire to dwell in His people.
  This is why God commanded them to erect the Tabernacle
  in their midst whenever they pitched camp.

- The various barriers around and within the Tabernacle pictured the fact that the Israelites were separated from God because of their sinfulness.

- The High Priest pictured the fact that God would provide a Mediator to rectify the Israelites' sin-problem.

- The animal sacrifices pictured the fact that God would provide a blameless Substitute whose death would pay for the guilt of their sins.

This elaborate ritualistic system was an effective instructional device, but God never planned for it to be the permanent way His people should relate to Him. It was a temporary system that was to be fulfilled by Messiah's death, and then replaced by a new and better way of relating to God (see Jeremiah 31:31-34; Hebrews 7:11-10:18).

But now these "shadows" have been fulfilled by the "reality." Because Jesus' death has paid for all of our sins (Colossians 2:13,14), those who believe in Jesus are actually indwelt by Him through His Spirit. This is why Paul speaks of "Christ *in* you" in Colossians 1:27. Paul makes this same point in another letter:

> Galatians 4:[4] But when the fullness of the time came, God sent forth His Son, born of a woman, born under the Law, [5] so that He might redeem those who were under the Law, that we might receive the adoption as sons. [6] Because you are sons, God has sent forth the Spirit of His Son into our hearts, crying, "Abba! Father!"

Through His death, Jesus has provided complete forgiveness and adoption into God's family, so we can be indwelt by His Spirit and relate to Him personally as our "Abba" ("Papa"). The moment you receive Christ, God permanently gives you these gifts. You can relate to God wherever you are, secure in His love, sharing your problems and joys, thanking Him for His involvement in your life, and asking Him for the help you need. It's not just that there is now no *need* for ritualism; it's that ritualism now *interferes* with the development and enjoyment of your personal relationship with God.

This is why there is such a dramatic change in the role of biblical ritual before and after Jesus came. There were hundreds of prescribed rituals for God's people in the Old Testament, but there are only two since His death and resurrection. And one of these two rituals (baptism) is observed only once. There were detailed instructions on how to practice the Old Testament rituals (because of their symbolic significance), but there is very little New Testament instruction on how to practice baptism and communion. So little, in fact, that Christendom has tragically been fighting for centuries over how to practice them!

This is why Paul goes on to say to the Galatians that for Christians to revert to ritualism is not spiritual progress, but rather spiritual *regression.*

Galatians 4:[9] But now that you have come to know God, or rather to be known by God, how is it that you turn back again to the weak and worthless elemental things, to which you desire to be enslaved all over again? [10] You observe days and months and seasons and years. [11] I fear for you, that perhaps I have labored over you in vain.

Imagine a girl separated at birth from her father. She has only pictures of him, which she treasures and looks at daily. Then her father returns. Shouldn't she relate to the pictures differently now? She wouldn't hate them or throw them away, but she wouldn't relate to her father through them anymore. Now she can—and she should—build a relationship with him through regular personal interaction. What if she went back to relating to her father through her pictures? Wouldn't that be a tragedy? Wouldn't that communicate that her father's return was in vain?

So the New Testament is not positive, or even neutral, concerning ritualism. It is *against* ritualism. Ritualism is out of step with God's plan of salvation, it profoundly misrepresents Christianity to the watching world, and it will impede your own spiritual maturity.

True, Paul acknowledges that true Christians can and do practice ritualism. He urges us to love them as brothers and sisters who are weak in faith, rather than contemptuously judge them. He warns us not to shame them out of these practices, but rather to help them learn the above truths so they can relate to God non-ritualistically with a clear conscience (see Romans 14; 1 Corinthians 8). But, as you can see from Colossians 2:16,17, Paul warned already-instructed Christians to stay away from ritualism.

Mysticism

> [2.18] Let no one keep defrauding you of your prize by delighting in self-abasement and the worship of the angels, taking his stand on visions he has seen, inflated without cause by his fleshly mind.

Here is a second religious practice by which Christians are commonly drawn off the path to spiritual maturity. The false teachers were pronouncing the Colossian Christians "second class citizens" because they hadn't had certain dramatic spiritual experiences. These false teachers had evidently deprived themselves of food or sleep, or had even beaten themselves in order to induce an altered state of consciousness. They had so-called "visions" in which they either worshipped angelic beings or witnessed angels worshipping God. Because they had these experiences, they arrogantly claimed to have the "inside track" on God. They were evidently telling the Colossians that unless they had similar experiences, they would remain spiritual pygmies.

We may call this spiritual sidetrack *mysticism*. The term "mysticism" may refer broadly to the experiential aspect of our relationship with God, which is legitimate and important. But I am using "mysticism" negatively to refer to the error of *seeking dramatic experiences as a key to spiritual maturity.*

Mysticism is the dominant form of spirituality in the West today. Decades of atheistic naturalism discredited the Bible as an authoritative guide for knowing God. It also created a tremendous spiritual vacuum in people's hearts. As the light of biblical truth has declined, the false light of mysticism has grown. People rightly thirst for spiritual reality in their lives, but are vulnerable to all sorts of deceptive mysticism in an attempt to fill that spiritual vacuum. Transcendental Meditation, New Age channeling and spirit-guides, Native American vision quests, and other disciplines promise life-changing mystical experiences.

Even more disturbing is the vulnerability of true Christians (like the Colossians) to mysticism. The last few decades have witnessed wave after wave of so-called "spiritual revival" movements that promise dramatic spiritual experiences as the key to a victorious Christian life—experiences like speaking in tongues, being slain in the Spirit, and instantaneous inner healing. Some of these experiences, like being slain in the Spirit, have no biblical basis whatever. Others, like speaking in tongues and inner healing, have a biblical basis but distort the role of these experiences as we will see below.

Why was Paul so upset with these forms of mysticism? It wasn't because God never grants dramatic experiences to His people. Paul himself had seen the risen Christ at His conversion and several times afterward. He had been caught up to the very presence of God and heard things impossible and impermissible to describe (2 Corinthians 12:2-4). Certainly these qualify as dramatic spiritual experiences! Yet mysticism is spiritually dangerous for at least two reasons:

- Thirsting for dramatic spiritual experiences can lead us into spiritual deception and even into demonic bondage. The spiritual realm is real, but it is populated by deceiving spirits as well as by God and His angels. Demons can and do deliver powerful spiritual experiences, sometimes directly and sometimes through false teachers. Jesus warned that false prophets would come in His name and deceive even true Christians through their miraculous signs and wonders (Matthew 7:15-23; 24:11,24). The Antichrist will exert an unparalleled deluding influence through his satanically-empowered miracles (2 Thessalonians 2:9-12). So an undiscerning lust for dramatic spiritual experiences exposes us to extreme spiritual peril!

- Having genuine (God-given) dramatic spiritual experiences can lead us to wrongly conclude that we are spiritually mature. But there is no biblical connection between the two. The Corinthian Christians had all kinds of genuine dramatic spiritual experiences, yet Paul calls them immature because they lack the proof of spiritual maturity—serving love (1 Corinthians 3:3). On the other hand, many Christians become spiritually mature, loving servants of Jesus without ever having dramatic spiritual experiences.

Some Christians over-react against mysticism by rejecting healthy spiritual experience. The result is an almost exclusively cognitive and functional aberration that is just as unhealthy as mysticism. Paul's two-fold antidote to mysticism is a relationally healthy Christian life.

2,19 (These people are) not holding fast to the Head, from whom the entire body, being supplied and held together by the joints and ligaments, grows with a growth which is from God.

- "Holding fast to the Head" means to *build your relationship with Christ through the Bible.* Paul uses this same verb (*krateo*) in 2 Thessalonians 2:15, where he urges the Thessalonian Christians to "hold fast to the teachings we passed on to you, whether by word of mouth or by letter." These "teachings" are the message of Jesus through His apostles, preserved for us in the New Testament. Mysticism leads us beyond or away from Jesus' message—but in biblical Christianity, Jesus reveals Himself to us and mediates His spiritual life to us through His words (John 6:63). Holding fast to Jesus' Word not only protects us from spiritual deception; it also personally nourishes our souls (1 Timothy 4:6).

- "Being supplied and held together by the joints and ligaments" means to *build and maintain Christ-centered friendships with other Christians.* Paul uses this same physical body analogy in another letter:

Ephesians 4:14 As a result, we are no longer to be children, tossed here and there by waves and carried about by every wind of doctrine, by the trickery of men, by craftiness in deceitful scheming; 15 but speaking the truth in love, we are to grow up in all aspects into Him who is the head, even Christ, 16from whom the whole body, being fitted and held together by what every joint supplies, according to the proper working of each individual part, causes the growth of the body for the building up of itself in love.

God both protects us from spiritual deception and nourishes us into healthy growth as we "speak the truth in love" to one another. "Supplied," "held together," and "fitted together" all describe an ongoing vital linkage with other Christians. Mysticism leads to thinking that "I am so close to God that you don't need His people"—but biblical Christianity leads to relying on His people to communicate His love and truth to us.

The result of relating to Christ in this way is genuine growth from God—gradual growth in your personal relationship with Him and in your ability to love others!

Legalism

[2,20] If you have died with Christ to the elementary principles of the world, why, as if you were living in the world, do you submit yourself to decrees, such as, [21] "Do not handle, do not taste, do not touch!" [22] (which all refer to things destined to perish with use)—in accordance with the commandments and teachings of men?

The false teachers told the Colossians that it was wrong to eat certain foods—and that following these prohibitions was therefore required for spirituality. This is an example of *legalism*. Christians use this term in many ways, but I am using here to refer to *an emphasis on man-made rules and prohibitions as a requirement of spirituality.*

Legalism is a prominent feature of most world religions. Dietary restrictions, dress codes, isolation from "unclean" people, prescribed fasts, and celibacy are key features of the "spiritual life" in most religious traditions.

Tragically, these same forms of legalism have dominated most versions of Christianity, even though Jesus and the apostles directly opposed them. Some monastic traditions exalt the legalistic life as the "spiritual life." American fundamentalism's many extra-biblical prohibitions (forbidding drinking alcohol, watching secular movies, playing cards, wearing dresses and make-up, listening to secular music, dancing, etc.) has created a sub-culture that Jesus never intended.

The intent of legalism is to protect us from sin: "Since X is sinful, it is spiritual to have a rule against activities that might tempt us to do X." Legalism says: "Since drunkenness is sinful, then it is spiritual to prohibit drinking alcohol or going places where people get drunk." Legalism says: "Since sexual immorality is sinful, then it is spiritual to prohibit watching movies or reading books that include any form of sexual immorality."

What's wrong with legalism? On one level, it takes morality seriously, and it seems to provide safeguards against sin. Paul, like Jesus (see Mark 7:8-13), rejects it because it goes beyond God's Word. It is merely "in accordance with the commandments and teachings of men." To make moral rules that God never prescribed, and to communicate that He did make these rules, is to usurp God's authority. Consider some of the disastrous consequences of this error:

- Legalism needlessly alienates non-Christians. It misrepresents God as a Cosmic Killjoy instead of the Giver of Abundant Life. It implies that we have to clean ourselves up morally before we can come to Christ, instead of coming to Him as we are and allowing Him to change us from the inside out. It creates ghettoes of finger-pointers instead of people like Jesus, who never compromised morally, but loved lost people and was known as "the friend of sinners."

- Legalism defines "worldliness" superficially. "Worldliness" in the New Testament is conformity to self-centered values like hedonism, materialism and

egotism (1 John 2:15,16). By defining "worldliness" in
extra-biblical behavioral terms, legalism actually
justifies worldliness! Jesus rebukes the legalistic
Pharisees for meticulously observing their many
restrictions while egotistically loving people's respectful
greetings and materialistically preying on widows'
property (Matthew 23:5-7,14). Haven't you known
legalists who totally abstain from alcohol, but who are
deeply materialistic? Haven't you met legalists who are
pridefully self-righteous about their frugal lifestyle? It
is one thing to be worldly and know it; it is quite
another to be worldly and think you are spiritual!

- Legalism defines spiritual maturity negatively ("What I
  don't/can't do") instead of positively ("How I love and
  serve others"). It focuses people on impersonal rule-
  keeping instead of on how to help people meet Christ
  and grow in Him. With a love-focus, we have the
  freedom to thankfully enjoy God's good gifts within His
  ethical absolutes, but we are willing to *not* use these
  freedoms out of love to help people
  (1 Corinthians 10:23 – "All things are lawful for me,
  but not all things build up others"). We are also able to
  refrain from these freedoms when the Holy Spirit shows
  us that we are not presently able to handle them
  (1 Corinthians 6:12 – "All things are lawful for me, but
  I will not be mastered by anything"), but without
  making them rules that everybody else has to obey.

Summing up

Paul summarizes his critique of these three religious practices in
2:23.

2.23 These are matters which have, to be sure, the appearance
of wisdom in self-made religion and self-abasement and
severe treatment of the body, but are of no value against
fleshly indulgence.

What an insightful critique! Ritualism, mysticism and legalism may
look outwardly impressive, but they are impotent to fix the real
problem – our "fleshly indulgence," or self-centeredness.[1] In fact,
they tend to promote self-righteous pride, which is the most
dangerous form of self-centeredness! No wonder Paul warns us to
steer clear of religious practices. They lead people away from
authentic spiritual maturity and toward a counterfeit form of
spirituality.

But what is authentic spiritual maturity, and what is the way that
leads toward it? Paul answers these questions in Colossians 3,4.

---

[1] "Fleshly" here probably does not refer to our "physical bodies;" it refers to our fallen, selfish
nature. "Indulgence" means gratifying that selfish nature.

Chapter 9
Colossians 3:1-4
The Path to Spiritual Maturity — Part #1

In Colossians 3, Paul shifts from warning the Colossians about counterfeit spiritualities to instructing them on God's pathway to spiritual maturity. In the previous paragraph (2:16-23), he counseled: "Stay away from religious 'short-cuts' because they are blind alleys that will lead you away from true spiritual maturity." Now he explains the proper path to spiritual maturity. The first step down this path may seem impractical—even counter-intuitive—but it unleashes God's power to radically renovate our lives. This step is a mental focus on what Paul calls "the things above."

3:1 Therefore if you have been raised up with Christ, keep seeking the things above, where Christ is, seated at the right hand of God. 2 Set your mind on the things above, not on the things that are on earth. 3 For you have died and your life is hidden with Christ in God. 4 When Christ, who is our life, is revealed, then you also will be revealed with Him in glory.

"The things above"

The term "the things above" doesn't refer to physical things in the sky, such as the sun or the moon or the stars. Rather, it refers to the things that originate from God—specifically, the things He says about Jesus and what He has provided for us. These "things" include certain amazing facts, including:

- Jesus is the Messiah who has physically conquered death and has full authority over sin, death and Satan. Verse 1

describes Jesus as "Christ," God's victorious King who has
been raised from the dead. It also describes Him as now
"seated at the right hand of God." This is a figure of speech
which refers to being in the position of favor and authority
(see Ephesians 1:20,21).[1]

- We who belong to Jesus are already fundamentally different
  persons through our union with Him. Verse 1 implies that
  we now have access to Christ's authority (see also Ephesians
  1:20,21; 2:6). Verse 3 says that we have "died" to who we
  were before, and verse 1 says that we have been "raised" to
  new life with Christ. In fact, verse 4 says that Christ now "is
  our life." As we saw in Colossians 2:10-15, this new life
  includes complete forgiveness, deliverance from sin's
  authority, and deliverance from demonic domination.

- We will one day share the glory of Jesus. Verse 3 says that in
  this life, our union with Him is not presently physically
  visible—it is "hidden" from sight. But verse 4 says that on
  the day when Christ returns in His glorious resurrected
  body, He will transform us so that we also will have
  glorious resurrected bodies (see also 1 John 3:2;
  Philippians 3:20,21).

There are many other "things above" that are revealed in other
biblical passages—including God's plan for humanity, our unique
roles in His plan, and the gift of His Spirit (see Ephesians 1:3-14).
Fallen human society is blind to these "things" or their value—but
they are true and real, and God will vindicate them when all else
passes away.

---

[1] "Seated" may also allude to the fact that Jesus has finished His redemptive work of
purchasing our salvation through His death on the cross. See Hebrews 1:3 for this same sense
– " ...when he had made purification of sins, He sat down at the right hand of the Majesty on
high" (see Colossians 2:10-15).

By contrast, we could focus on "the things that are on earth." This term doesn't refer to physical things like trees, mountains, oceans, animals, and other people. Rather, it refers to the things that originate from fallen humans.

- In the preceding context, Paul refers to religious and philosophical teachings and practices that originate not from God, but from fallen humans and deceiving spirits. He calls these teachings and practices "the elementary principles of the world" (see 2:8,20). They contradict what God says about Jesus' identity and what He has provided for us. These "things," no matter how spiritual they may seem, are of no true spiritual value (2:23). These "things" will not help us toward spiritual maturity, but instead will "delude" us (2:4) and "take us captive" (2:8).

- In the following context, Paul refers to a self-centered lifestyle—sexual self-centeredness (3:5), monetary self-centeredness (3:5), and relational self-centeredness (3:8,9). These "things," no matter how glamorously the world portrays them, are the antithesis of real spiritual maturity— a lifestyle of other-centered, sacrificial love.

So Paul is saying: "If you want to grow toward spiritual maturity, you must cultivate a mental focus on what God has provided for you through Jesus." This is exactly what he teaches in another passage:

And do not be conformed to this world, but be transformed *by* the renewing of your mind... (Romans 12:2)

What is it that unleashes God's power to gradually transform us? It is the "renewing of our minds"—thinking in a whole new way, or as Paul says in this passage, focusing on "the things above." Paul uses two different verbs here to describe related-but-distinct ways to cultivate this focus.

"Keep seeking the things above"

"Keep seeking" (*zeteo*) means "to inquire into; to find out by thinking, meditating, reasoning."[2] Jesus uses *zeteo* when He asks His disciples: "Are you *deliberating* together about (what I said)?" (John 16:19) "Keep seeking" is in the present tense, which emphasizes that this is something we are to continue to do. So Paul is saying: "Keep increasing in your understanding of God's provision through Jesus." Keep inquiring into it, keep thinking about it, keep reasoning about it, keep meditating on it. He is calling us to cultivate an insatiable spiritual curiosity—similar to (but far more important than) the curiosity that drives a scientific researcher to discover more and more about the subject of his research.

What God has given us through Jesus is so vast that we can never fully comprehend it, and it is so precious that we can never fully appreciate it. But an increasing comprehension and appreciation of God's gift is right at the core of a spiritually healthy life. This is what deepens our confidence and security in God and His love. This is what increases our gratitude to God. This is what fires our motivation to follow and serve God. This is what unleashes the Holy Spirit to form Christ's character in us.

Conversely, to lose this curiosity, to settle for the understanding you already have, to fade in your appreciation of this treasure so that you take it for granted is the most common cause of spiritual sickness in the Christian life. This creates a spiritual vacuum in your heart which ignites envy of other people, and lust for more money, possessions, and prestige. This is what leads you to use other people in various ways, and to dispose of them when they disappoint you.

How can we "keep seeking the things above?" God reveals "the things above" through the Bible, and especially through the New

---

[2] *Enhanced Strong's Lexicon.*

Testament since it expounds what God has given us through Jesus Christ. So "seeking the things above" involves ongoing exploration of biblical books like Colossians. There are many ways to do this.

- *Pray for God to increase your understanding and appreciation of what He has given you.* The Psalmist prays, "Open my eyes, that I may behold wonderful things in Your instruction" (Psalm 119:18). Paul prays for the Ephesian Christians that God may enlighten "the eyes of (their) hearts" to see what is theirs in Christ (Ephesians 1:18,19a). These "things" are not merely cognitive concepts; they are spiritual truths that require spiritual illumination. God has given us His Spirit "so that you might know the things He has freely given to us" (1 Corinthians 2:12). Do you pray for this whenever you expose yourself to biblical truth? Might it be true that you do not have because you do not ask?

- *Regularly listen to quality teachings and read quality books on God's provision through Christ.* Ask your Christian friends for suggestions. Read or listen carefully and prayerfully, asking God to increase your understanding, appreciation and application of His provisions in Christ. When you find a teaching or book that enriches you, deeply digest it by re-listening or re-reading. What was the last teaching or book that you digested in this way? Are you a lifelong learner of this most important subject?

- *Regularly discuss this subject with Christian friends who have the same aspiration.* "What provisions in God's Word have built you up lately?" is a great question to keep discussing. Such conversations will stimulate you in the best sense of the word. I meet with weekly with several Christian friends, and discussing the answer to this question is a big reason why these times are so refreshing and motivating. These conversations often lead me to other great teachings and books on this subject, and they will lead to great prayer together. Is this a regular part of your schedule? Who could you ask to do this with you?

- *Memorize and regularly meditate on key biblical passages on this subject.* Meditation is mentally "muttering" the very words of God so that your soul digests their nourishment. Charles Spurgeon said: "Meditation is of great value in opening up truth and leading us into (the Bible's) secrets... He who would be rich in these treasures must dig into scripture as one who seeks for choice pearls. You must go down into its depths, and you must rummage there until you get at last to the treasure... Cultivate much, then, the habit of... meditation, because of the way in which it opens up the truth."

   Take a small passage like this one (Colossians 3:1-4). Keep writing it down, or listening to it, or repeating it until you know it by heart. Then say it throughout the day, turning it into prayer. Turn its promises into prayers of thanks: "Thank You that I have been raised up with Christ. Thank You that I have died and my life is hidden with Christ in God. Thank You that when Christ appears, I will appear with Him in glory." As this brings to mind related promises, thank God for these also. Turn its commands into prayer requests: "Help me to keep seeking these things. Give me renewed thirst to do this. Help me to set my mind on these things. Teach me how to do this." As this brings to mind other related needs, ask God for these also.

   How I wish I could convince all of my brothers and sisters to memorize and meditate on biblical passages about God's provisions! This is a vanishing practice among American Christians, and we are forfeiting incalculable spiritual blessing because of our neglect. Build the habit of biblical meditation!

"Keep seeking the things above" is foundational to growth toward spiritual maturity. Just as foundational is Paul's command in 3:2— "set your mind on the things above"...

"Set your mind on the things above"

"Set your mind" (*phroneo*) means "to direct one's mind to a thing; to choose to adopt or maintain a point of view."[3] This verb implies a mental battle with opposing viewpoints that must be rejected or replaced. Thus, Paul says: "Set your mind on the things above, *not* on the things that are on earth." "Set your mind" is also in the present tense, so it is also something that we are to continue to do.

So while "keep seeking the things above" emphasizes the need to keep increasing your understanding of God's gift, "set your mind on the things above" emphasizes the need to keep identifying false thoughts and replacing them with the truth about what God has given you. Paul describes this as "mental combat" in another passage:

> We are destroying speculations and every lofty thing raised up against the knowledge of God, and we are taking every thought captive to the obedience of Christ... (2 Corinthians 10:5)

How aggressive this language is! Paul is referring in this passage to false teaching, but we are also to vigilantly monitor our own thought-lives. We are not to passively allow false thoughts and feelings to take us hostage. rather, we are to attack these lies and take them prisoner to the promises about God's provisions through Jesus.

J. I. Packer describes what this "mental combat" looks like in his classic book, *Knowing God*.

---

[3] *Enhanced Strong's Lexicon.*

"Think of what you know of God through the gospel, says Paul, and apply it. Think against your feelings; argue yourself out of the gloom they have spread; unmask the unbelief they have nourished; take yourself in hand, talk to yourself, make yourself look up from your problems to the God of the gospel; let *evangelical* (gospel-centered) thinking correct *emotional* thinking."[4]

D. M. Lloyd-Jones also describes it in his classic book, *Spiritual Depression*:

"Have you realized that most of your unhappiness in life is due to the fact that you are listening to yourself instead of talking to yourself? Take those thoughts that come to you the moment you wake up in the morning. You have not originated them, but they start talking to you, they bring back the problems of yesterday, etc. Somebody is talking. Who is talking to you? Your self is talking to you... You have to take yourself in hand, you have to address yourself, preach to yourself, question yourself... You must turn on yourself... exhort yourself, and say to yourself: 'Hope in God'—instead of muttering in this depressed unhappy way. And then you must go on to remind yourself of God, Who God is, and what God has done and what God has pledged Himself to do."[5]

What will help us to "set our minds on the things above?" Here are some steps that have been helpful to me:

- *Ask God to expose lies that are ingrained in your thinking.* David prays: "Search me, O God, and know my heart... see if there be any hurtful way within me" (Psalm 139:23,24).

---

[4] J. I. Packer, *Knowing God* (InterVarsity Press, 1973), p. 236.

[5] D. M. Lloyd-Jones, *Spiritual Depression: Its Causes and Cure* (Eerdmans, 1982), pp. 20,21.

God will usually answer this prayer in one of two ways. First, as you read and listen to God's Word, He will cause certain promises to "light up" and then challenge a cynical or despairing response to them. For example, you read Colossians 3:12, where Paul says that you are "chosen of God, set apart and beloved"—and realize that your mental response is: "Yeah, right – I am just a loser, a liability to God." Or you may read Romans 8:28, which says that "God causes all things to work together for good" for Christians—and realize that your mental response is: "God can't redeem the mess I've made of this situation." Alternatively, you might ask mature Christian friends who know you well: "Do you think I am in chronic unbelief about any of God's provisions? If so, which ones?" They will often have insight into lies you believe without even realizing it.

- *When you become aware of an "intruder" lie (a lie that is currently attacking you), verbalize it to God and then attack it by agreeing with what He says.* It is not enough to identify the lies that characterize your thought-life. By itself, this can be a very depressing realization! It is as we consciously verbalize these lies to God and then affirm to Him what He says that His Spirit gradually changes our character and brings life and peace to our souls (Romans 8:5-11). This past week, I have been beset daily by intensely fearful thoughts and feelings. On one level, these fearful thoughts and feelings are beyond my control. They emerge spontaneously because of things that are happening to me, and I can't just turn them off like a light switch. But on another level, I have a responsibility to pass judgment on the validity of these fearful thoughts and feelings in light of what God says. Hundreds of times in His Word, God says: "You don't need to succumb to fear, because I am with you."

Even though it takes conscious mental effort to answer each
fearful thought and feeling by affirming God's promise, this
is the way God has provided for me to overcome my fears.
The effort is real, but it is far less exhausting than constant
anxiety, and it leads back to the path of God's peace!

- *When you realize you have a "stronghold" lie (a lie that you
  have believed for years), ask your Christian friends to help
  you develop a strategy to combat this lie.* Such "strongholds"
  often take root in childhood, especially if you experienced
  chronic or severe neglect, abandonment, or abuse.
  "Stronghold" lies are self-defining lies (e.g., "I am without
  value unless I perform well;" "No one will protect me – I
  must protect myself at all costs;" "I will always fail").
  Believing these lies leads to developing strategies of survival
  (e.g., intimidation, isolation, posturing, self-sabotage, etc.).

These strategies "work" in that they help you to survive your
painful childhood. But after coming to faith in Christ, these
same strategies block deepening trust in God which is
necessary for spiritual growth. For example, I may have
protected myself from humiliation by always putting my
best foot forward, but this is no longer necessary now that
God is my loving Father—He knows the worst about me, yet
He accepts me fully. Now my posturing blocks God from
giving me a growing security in His love.

As God unearths these lies and exposes our survival
strategies, we need to choose to affirm what God says in this
area despite deep-seated thoughts and feelings to the
contrary. Sometimes God exposes and breaks these
strongholds in quick and dramatic ways. More often,
exposure and healing involve a gradual process.

A friend of mine suffered horrible verbal and physical abuse by one of his parents. His earliest memories are of being beaten and told, "I hate you and I wish you were never born!" As a young teenager, he vowed to himself never to let anyone have any control over him. This "worked" in that it prevented further abuse, but it also led to a life of destructive anger and many other problems, including alcohol abuse.

When he received Christ as an adult, he experienced forgiveness and new hope for his life. But his commitment to stay in control of his life prevented him from building close friendships and consistently serving others. Through Christian friends, he has begun to realize that his survival strategy is counter-productive. He has found that memorizing passages like Psalm 23 remind him that God is now his Father who takes care of him. Because of this, he does not have to control his environment and protect himself from all relational pain. He is starting to open up to Christian friends and serve people.

His Christian friends pray with him for this area of his life and have helped him to forgive and confront his abusive parent. They also challenge him to keep going down this path when he wants to revert to his old survival strategy. It is a daily battle for him to reject this lie and live like God's child. He often gets discouraged and needs reminders of how far God has brought him. But he is slowly learning how to trust God and love others!

More is involved in growing toward spiritual maturity. Paul describes another crucial step in Colossians 3:5-11. But the *foundation* of all healthy spiritual growth is what we just learned.

Lay this foundation well, and you will be able to build upon it with God's power. Neglect it, and whatever you build will crumble!

Chapter 10
Colossians 3:5-17
The Path to Spiritual Maturity — Part #2

In the previous chapter, we learned that the path to spiritual maturity begins with cultivating a mental focus on what God has provided for us through Christ. As we keep increasing our understanding and appreciation of these provisions, and as we use these provisions to refute and replace lies about who God is and who we are, the power of the Holy Spirit gradually transforms us.

In addition to cultivating this mental focus on God's provisions, the path to spiritual maturity also involves embracing a new lifestyle—a new purpose and direction for our lives. This is what Paul describes in Colossians 3:5-17. He likens our old lifestyle to an old set of clothes we are to "put aside," and this new lifestyle to a new set of clothes we are to "put on."

Put aside the self-centered lifestyle

> [3:5] Therefore consider the members of your earthly body as dead to immorality, impurity, passion, evil desire, and greed, which amounts to idolatry. [6] For it is because of these things that the wrath of God will come upon the sons of disobedience, [7] and in them you also once walked, when you were living in them. [8] But now you also, *put them all aside:* anger, wrath, malice, slander, and abusive speech from your mouth. [9] Do not lie to one another, since you laid aside the old self with its evil practices, [10] and have put on the new self who is being renewed to a true knowledge according to

> the image of the One who created him— [11] a renewal in
> which there is no distinction between Greek and Jew,
> circumcised and uncircumcised, barbarian, Scythian, slave
> and freeman, but Christ is all, and in all.

Paul describes different kinds of behaviors that characterize this old
lifestyle: sexual immorality (3:5), materialistic greed (3:5), and
relationally destructive interactions (3:8,9a). But it is important to
understand that the heart of all of these behaviors is a *self-centered*
orientation to life.[1] Paul describes this self-centered orientation as
"evil desire" in Colossians 3:5. Desire is not evil in itself; it is self-
centered craving or lust that is wrong. The old lifestyle is like a
sucking vortex—an emptiness that takes from other people and
things in order to become full. It is this orientation that leads to:

- *Sexual* taking: "I need to feel pleasure," or "I need to be
  wanted," or "I need to needed"—so we use our sexuality to
  get these things through pornography, sexual promiscuity,
  serial romances, marital infidelity, etc.

- *Materialistic* greed: "I need to feel materially secure," or "I
  need to feel stimulated by new acquisitions," or "I need to
  feel significant through career accomplishment"—so we
  use money and possessions and career to get these things.

- *Relational* demandingness: "I need people to treat me in
  certain ways so that I feel secure, important, appreciated,
  etc."—so we explode or simmer in destructive anger to
  punish those who don't meet our demands, or we lie in
  various ways in order to extract from other people what we
  believe we must have.

Human beings have been self-centered ever since Adam and Eve
kicked God out of their lives and turned away from trusting Him to

---

[1] See previous footnote on "fleshly indulgence" in Colossians 2:23.

meet their needs. That's when the "sucking sound" in our souls began, and that's what gives birth to these specific behaviors.

Our culture is certainly not the first culture to be selfish, but it may be the first culture to view selfishness as a virtue and a key feature of psychological health. This is why the Bible's denunciation of selfishness seems so implausible to us. So we need to understand the *reasons* Paul gives us for turning away from it. We should put it aside because:

God will judge it.

> [3:6] For it is because of these things that the wrath of God will come upon the sons of disobedience...

Many teachers use this verse as a threat that God will damn Christians to hell if they commit sexual immorality. Interestingly, they don't usually threaten this for materialism! This is a terrible misinterpretation because it directly contradicts Paul's teaching in this same letter (along with many other biblical passages) that Christians are permanently exempt from God's condemnation (see Colossians 1:14; 2:13,14; 3:4). Rather, Paul is saying that God's wrath is going to come upon "the sons of disobedience"—the people who refuse to receive Christ's gift of forgiveness. Paul's logic is: "You are headed for eternity in God's kingdom, not for His judgment. Why would you want to live like those who are headed for His judgment?"

We have already tried living this way.

> [3:7]... and in them you also once walked, when you were living in them.

Did a self-centered lifestyle ever fulfill you? If it was so fulfilling, why did you come to Christ? This is why Paul asks in Romans 6:21, "What benefit were you then deriving from the things of which you are now ashamed? For the outcome of those things is death." Isn't it true that this way of life never fulfilled you, always left you empty, enslaved you, and damaged you and others? If one form of selfishness did this, why would another form be any different? If there is now an alternative to this way of life, why wouldn't you want to take it?

It no longer fits who we are.

> [3.9] Do not lie to one another, since you laid aside the old self with its evil practices, [10] and have put on the new self...

Paul's call to "put off" a self-centered way of life is rooted in the fact that Christians have a new identity. I don't wear clothes that I wore fifty years ago, because they no longer fit who I am. Rather, I wear clothes that fit my present size and tastes because they express who I now am. In the same way, I received a new identity when I received Christ. My old identity as an orphan and fugitive from God is gone; I am now a child of God who is loved and fully cared for by Him. Therefore, it makes no sense to live a self-centered, self-protective, taking lifestyle.

We now have access to God's changing power.

> [3.10] (you) have put on the new self who is being renewed to a true knowledge according to the image of the One who created him...

Before, we had no power to change—we were slaves to selfishness. But now, through Christ, we've been released from sin's authority and God's Spirit lives within us. He is constantly initiating a renovation to restore us to live the way God designed us to live.

Real, increasing freedom from self-centeredness begins not with moral will-power, but with deepened convictions about these reasons for change. What self-centered way of life is appealing to you right now? Do you agree with God that it is ultimately unfulfilling and incongruous with whom you are? Do you believe that God's Spirit has the power to free you from it? If so, tell Him that you agree with Him, and then ask Him to show you how He wants to lead you away from this trap. He will give you a step to take—and if you take it, He will begin to break its power over you.

But "putting aside" is never sufficient. When we only try to "put aside"—even for all the right reasons—we never succeed. This is because we have a "fulfillment vacuum" in our hearts which, unless it is filled by another lifestyle, sucks us back into some form of self-centeredness. We don't want to exchange sexual selfishness for materialistic selfishness, nor do we want to exchange secular career selfishness for church career selfishness. Rather, we want to exchange selfishness for a radically new orientation toward life. This is why in addition to "putting aside" a self-centered lifestyle, we need to "put on" the new lifestyle that fits who we now are in Christ. The more we embrace this new lifestyle, the more we experience the real fulfillment that our hearts rightly desire, the easier it is to believe who we are in Christ—and the less attractive a selfish lifestyle becomes. This is exactly what we want—real, lasting, and satisfying lifestyle change!

Put on a lifestyle of love

> [3,12] So, as those who have been chosen of God, holy and beloved, *put on* a heart of compassion, kindness, humility, gentleness and patience; [13] bearing with one another, and forgiving each other, whoever has a complaint against anyone; just as the Lord forgave you, so also should you. [14] Beyond all these things *put on* love, which is the perfect bond of unity. [15] Let the peace of Christ rule in your hearts, to which indeed you were called in one body; and be thankful. [16] Let the word of Christ richly dwell within you,

with all wisdom teaching and admonishing one another
with psalms and hymns and spiritual songs, singing with
thankfulness in your hearts to God. [17] Whatever you do in
word or deed, do all in the name of the Lord Jesus, giving
thanks through Him to God the Father.

The center of the old lifestyle is self-centeredness. The center of the
new lifestyle is love: "Beyond all these things put on love." "Beyond"
means "above all," "over-arching all." Love is the central lifestyle
choice of which the other qualities in this passage are specific
expressions.

"Love" is the Greek word *agape*. The New Testament authors use this
word to describe the kind of love that Jesus demonstrated
throughout His life and supremely through His death. This love is
very different than other kinds of human love:

- It is not just enjoying people you already know, or who are
  like you. It is serving people you do not know, or who are
  very different from you. Jesus served and died for people
  who were very, very different from Him!

- It is not rooted in feelings of attraction. It is rooted in choice
  and commitment in spite of how you may feel. Jesus served
  people in spite of extreme weariness, and He went to the
  cross despite great fear and revulsion.

- It is not dependent on people treating you well. It forgives
  and serves even those who treat you badly. Jesus went to the
  cross for His enemies.

If you're thinking: "This way of life sounds crazy," it is only because
we are so conditioned to self-centeredness that it seems normal to
us. If you're thinking: "This way of life sounds impossible," you're
right—it is humanly impossible because *agape* comes only from
God, not from within us. But here is an amazing truth: The moment

you entrust yourself to Christ as your Savior, God's Spirit indwells your soul and gives you access to His love (Romans 5:5). His love toward you is utterly trustworthy and inexhaustible. Because of this access to God's love, you can begin to give His love away to others without fear of being left empty.

Here is an even more amazing truth: The more you give God's love away to others, the more His love fills your soul. This is why Jesus taught that "It is more fulfilling to give than it is to receive" (Acts 20:35). How liberating this is! No longer do we have to seek fulfillment by trying to get other people to treat us the way we want to be treated. Instead, we can be fulfilled by freely giving to others the love that God has freely given to us (Matthew 10:8). Therefore, the only thing that can stop us from being fulfilled is our unwillingness to love!

Do you believe that God loves you and will meet all of your needs through Christ (Philippians 4:19)? Do you believe that true fulfillment comes from giving God's love away to others? Many true Christians never experience growth toward spiritual maturity simply because they do not believe these two truths. But your spiritual life will change profoundly when you decide to believe them.

If you do believe these truths, you need to cooperate with God in building a lifestyle of love. Paul calls on us to do this by practicing love in three relational directions—*upward* (loving God by cultivating thankfulness to Him – 3:15b,16b,17b), *inward* (loving other Christians by building unified relationships with them – 3:12-16a), and *outward* (loving non-Christians by showing and sharing Christ's love with them – 3:17-4:6). Each of these is so important that we will spend the next few chapters looking at them in-depth.

God wants us to cultivate a "healthy addiction" to this way of life. Do you remember how you cultivated a destructive addiction? I remember how I did this with drugs. First, I participated in the activity. Then, I experienced the "high." Next, I began to build my life increasingly around getting high. Then, I needed more drugs to get the same high. And then I experienced the negative consequences of this lifestyle—lying, ripping people off, boredom and restlessness. Cultivating a healthy addiction to love-giving follows a similar pattern—but it leads to a very different result! Instead of enslaving and corrupting you, you will *thrive* off of this lifestyle because of the increasing joy and fulfillment it provides. Tell God that this is the kind of lifestyle you want, and ask Him to lead you into it. Then get ready for a life-long adventure that you will never regret!

Chapter 11
Colossians 3:15-17
The Path to Spiritual Maturity — Part #3

Embracing a Lifestyle of Love: Loving God through Thankfulness

As we have seen in the previous two chapters, Paul's instruction on how to grow toward spiritual maturity consists of two main parts. Foundationally, we need to cultivate a mental focus on what God has provided for us through Christ (Colossians 3:1-4). Then we need to embrace a lifestyle consistent with what God has provided for us through Christ (Colossians 3:5-17). This means putting aside a lifestyle of self-centeredness and putting on a lifestyle of biblical love. Paul says that this loving lifestyle is directed toward three relational foci: God, one another and people who don't know Christ.

In this chapter we will look more closely at loving God through thankfulness. Paul emphasizes its importance by urging it three times in three consecutive verses.

> [3:15] Let the peace of Christ rule in your hearts, to which indeed you were called in one body; and *be thankful.* [16] Let the word of Christ richly dwell within you, with all wisdom teaching and admonishing one another with psalms and hymns and spiritual songs, *singing with thankfulness in your hearts to God.* [17] Whatever you do in word or deed, do all in the name of the Lord Jesus, *giving thanks through Him to God the Father.*

Let's explore this key aspect of spiritual growth by asking three questions: What is biblical thankfulness? Why is it so important? How can we practically cultivate it?

What is biblical thankfulness?

Biblical thankfulness is different in several ways from the generic thankfulness of American culture. As we explore these differences, we will also note other passages in Colossians in which Paul emphasizes thanksgiving.

- Generic thankfulness is directed to people only, or to a vague God or "higher power." Biblical thankfulness does indeed include giving thanks to other people, but it is primarily thankful to the God of the Bible as the Source of all good gifts.

[1,3] We *give thanks* to God, the Father of our Lord Jesus Christ...

- Generic thankfulness is almost exclusively for temporal and material blessings, such as plentiful food and good health. Biblical thankfulness includes thankfulness for these things, but it focuses especially on God's gift of salvation through Jesus. God gives us these blessing the moment we receive Christ, and they are permanent and far greater in magnitude than temporal blessings.

[1,11]... joyously [12] *giving thanks* to the Father, who has qualified us to share in the inheritance of the saints in Light. [13] For He rescued us from the domain of darkness, and transferred us to the kingdom of His beloved Son, [14] in whom we have redemption, the forgiveness of sins.

- Generic thankfulness is usually reserved for certain special occasions, such as Thanksgiving or Christmas. Biblical thankfulness affirms special occasions, but it emphasizes developing a lifestyle and disposition of thankfulness.

[2,7] ... having been firmly rooted and now being built up in Him and established in your faith, just as you were instructed, and (continuously) *overflowing with gratitude.*

[3,15] Let the peace of Christ rule in your hearts... (continuously) *be thankful.*
[16] Let the word of Christ richly dwell within you... (continuously) *singing with thankfulness in your hearts to God.*
[17] Whatever you do in word or deed, do all in the name of the Lord Jesus, (continuously) *giving thanks through Him to God the Father.*

- Generic thankfulness is rooted in feelings of gratitude. Some people even think that it is inauthentic to give thanks unless you feel thankful. But biblical thankfulness is rooted in choice based on what is true regardless of our current feelings. This is why the phrases in Colossians 3:15-17 above are imperatives—commands to choose to give thanks. Seen in this way, thankfulness is a key expression of faith in God in the face of opposing circumstances or feelings.

- Most people do not view generic thankfulness as crucial to spirituality. But God asserts in several ways that biblical thankfulness is a key priority. The New Testament urges Christians to be thankful over forty times. Virtually everyone would agree that prayer is crucial to spirituality, but notice how Paul says our prayers should be laced with thankfulness.

[4,2] Devote yourselves to prayer, keeping alert in it with *an attitude of thanksgiving...*

1 Thessalonians 4:[17] Pray without ceasing; [18] in everything give thanks; for this is God's will for you in Christ Jesus.

This raises the second question: Why is thankfulness so important? Cultivating thankfulness is a challenge, so you will need to be convinced of its importance in order to take up this challenge.

Why is thankfulness so important?

Before we look at some of the biblical answers to this question, we need to reject a common-but-wrong reason: "Because God needs our thanksgiving." Unlike other gods, the God of the Bible is not some insecure Deity who needs to be constantly affirmed by having people thank Him. God is fully sufficient within Himself; He needs nothing from us.

He gives because it is His nature to give. He commands our thankfulness, not because He needs it, but because we need it. When our daughters eventually thanked me and my wife for parenting them in certain ways, we were happy—not because it validated us as parents, but because it showed that they were maturing.

Here are four biblical reasons why thankfulness is important:

- *Thankfulness is the only sane response to God's grace.* When my oldest daughter was four, I heard her screaming in her bedroom. When investigated, I saw her standing in front of her wardrobe shouting: "I don't have anything to wear!" I realized that she was just having a temporary fit of insanity. Her wardrobe was full of clothes to wear—but she was so focused on a dress she didn't have that she was temporarily detached from reality.

  That incident became an instructive parable for me. I realized that when I am unthankful, I am spiritually insane. I deserve God's judgment every day for my rebellion against Him. But instead of giving me what I deserve, He sent His Son to die for me. He has forgiven me completely, He has made me His beloved child, He has guaranteed that I'll be with Him for eternity, and He has given me His Spirit to encourage and empower me every step of the way until then. All these gifts are completely undeserved, they meet my deepest needs, and they are mine forever!

One of my friends says: "Every day I wake up and I'm not in hell is a good day!" Does that sound morbid to you? Actually, it is the mind-set of a thoroughly sane person! Thankfulness is a key way to "keep seeking" and "set my mind on" the things above (Colossians 3:1-4). The more I thank God for all He has given me through Christ, the more I am able to appreciate what He has given me. The more I thank God for this, the easier it is to combat lies about who God is and who I am.

- *Thankfulness is key to putting aside a self-centered lifestyle.* In the previous chapter, we saw that sinful behaviors like sexual immorality, materialistic greed, and relational demandingness are all rooted in a self-centered orientation toward life. Self-centeredness is essentially unthankful. An unthankful person feels empty and entitled, which breeds envy, jealousy, self-pity, etc.—and these attitudes breed sinful behaviors and habits that corrupt and enslave us and damage others.

That's why we have to attack these sinful behaviors on a deeper level than just trying to resist or avoid them. Ingratitude is the mother of sinful attitudes and behaviors, and gratitude is the mother of godly attitudes and behaviors. That's what Paul is getting at in another passage:

Romans 1:21 For even though they knew God, they did not honor Him as God or *give thanks*, but they became futile in their speculations, and their foolish heart was darkened... [23] and (they) exchanged the glory of the incorruptible God for an image (idolatry)... [24] Therefore God gave them over in the lusts of their hearts to impurity...

Notice that it is the refusal to thank God for who He is that starts humans' slide downward into selfish lifestyles that are enslaving and destructive. Martin Luther, commenting on this passage, says: "See, then, how great an evil ingratitude is: it produces a love of vanity; and this results in blindness, and blindness in idolatry, and idolatry brings about a whole host of vices."[1]

Conversely, Nancy DeMoss says: "So powerful is the influence exerted by ingratitude, that when we displace it with gratitude, we will likely find a multitude of other sins dislodged from our lives..."[2]

Do you battle recurrent temptation to sexual lust, materialism, and destructive relational sins like Paul describes in Colossians 3:5,8,9? Work hard (asking God's help) to practice thanksgiving, and discover how God works through it to weaken these temptations!

- *Thankfulness leads to loving other people more.* The Bible says that effectively loving other people (along with loving God) is the purpose of our existence and the definition of success (1 Corinthians 13:1-3). Thankfulness helps us in this direction in two ways: First, thankfulness provides motivation to be a giver rather than a taker. The more you think like a deprived and entitled person, the more you will relate to people as a taker. But the more you thank God for all He has

[1] Martin Luther, quoted in David W. Pao, *Thanksgiving: An Investigation of a Pauline Theme* (InterVarsity Press, 2002), p. 98.

[2] Nancy Leigh DeMoss, *Choosing Gratitude* (Moody Publishers, 2009), pp. 56,57.

given you, the more you will realize that you are His
well-loved child—and the more plausible and
appealing it is to give to others freely.
Second, thankfulness attracts people to us so that we
have more opportunities to love. Negative, bitter,
complaining, and self-pitying people have a repelling
effect on the people who interact with them. But
grateful people attract others into their winsome sphere
of influence. This attractiveness provides many
opportunities to serve and to become a more effective
servant—which is the life-goal of those who want to
grow toward spiritual maturity!

- *Thankfulness leads to increasing personal fulfillment.*
  Jack Miller said: "How happy a person is depends upon
  the depth of his gratitude."[3] Why is this? Consider some
  of the ways the Bible connects thankfulness with
  personal well-being.

Philippians 4.6 Be anxious for nothing, but in everything by
prayer and supplication *with thanksgiving* let your requests
be made known to God.
[7] And the peace of God, which surpasses all comprehension,
will guard your hearts and your minds in Christ Jesus.

As we combat our anxious thoughts and feelings by choosing to give
thanks to God for His promises (along with asking Him for help),
God's Spirit mysteriously mediates His peace to that guard our hearts
and minds in the midst of negative circumstances.
The Greek words for "grace" (*charis*), "give thanks"
(*eucharisto/chairo*) and "joy" (*chara*) are all related. This is more
than a coincidence. God's grace invites our gratitude as the only

---

[3] Jack Miller, cited by Ajith Fernando, *The Fullness of Christ* (Keswick Ministries, 2007), p. 89.

sane response.[4] And as we give thanks to God more and more for His grace, the Holy Spirit ignites more and more joy in our souls. For this reason:

> "Over time, choosing gratitude means choosing joy. But that choice doesn't come without effort and intentionality. It's a choice that requires constantly renewing my *mind* with the truth of God's Word, setting my *heart* to savor God and His gifts, and disciplining my *tongue* to speak words that reflect His grace and goodness—until a grateful spirit becomes my reflexive response to all of life."[5]

So there are at least four biblical reasons why cultivating thankfulness is so important. Don't rush over these reasons. If you aren't convinced they are true, ponder them and the scriptures connected to them, asking God to convince you. If you are convinced, then you need to address the next question...

How can we cultivate thankfulness?

"Cultivate" implies ongoing intentional activity. I am an amateur gardener, and I know the connection between my willingness to cultivate my plants and a good harvest. Fruitful gardeners differ widely in their cultivation schedules and styles—but they all cultivate diligently! Ask God to show you how to cultivate your own style of thankfulness. In that spirit, I offer here examples from my own thankfulness-cultivation strategy.

- I ask God to sensitize me to self-pity, complaining, etc. It is easy to gradually drift into an unthankful mind-set without

---

[4] "The fact that *charis* and *eucharistia* share the same stem has been noted by many. In the context of Pauline theology, the two words point to the same fundamental premise. Divine grace and the constant call to thanksgiving in Paul points to an undeserving act that alters one's fundamental orientation and relationship with God." David W. Pao, *Thanksgiving: An Investigation of a Pauline Theme* (InterVarsity Press, 2002), pp. 81,82.

[5] Nancy Leigh DeMoss, *Choosing Gratitude* (Moody Publishers, 2009), p. 17.

realizing it. When I ask God to show me this hurtful way,
He is faithful to do so. Then I try to respond in the following
ways.

- I try to appreciate my temporal blessings—starting with the
  amazing gift of being allowed to exist at all, and then by
  thanking God for whatever temporal blessing I presently
  notice. Some days, all I can muster is something pretty lame
  like: "Thank You that the sun is shining." I try to work from
  there to other temporal blessings that I tend to take for
  granted, like my physical health or my key relationships.
  The goal here is to notice and appreciate these blessings
  more than the circumstantial difficulties in my life.

- I focus especially on my spiritual blessings—mainly by
  memorizing and meditating on biblical passages that speak
  of these blessings. Passages like Romans 5:1-5,
  Ephesians 1:3-14, Psalm 23, and Romans 8 are some of my
  favorites. These blessings meet my deepest needs, and God
  says He has already permanently met them. The goal here is
  to keep deepening my understanding and appreciation of
  these greatest of gifts.

- I often begin times of private prayer with thanksgiving for
  the blessings stated above. I've noticed that in Paul's letters,
  he always thanks God *before* He petitions God. I find that
  doing this often lifts me out of negativity and mild
  depression, and that it leads to petitions that don't turn into
  more anxiety or negativity. So when I walk my dog daily, I
  try to make the first half of the walk thanksgiving, and then
  petition God during the second half.

- I usually give thanks to God for something before I get out of
  bed in the morning, and before I fall asleep at night. This

helps to combat the morning waterfall of accusatory and anxious thoughts, and it is a great way to fall asleep!

- When negativity besieges me so that I am unable to pull out of it, I admit this to another brother or sister and ask for help. They can remind me of my blessings and pray with me to give thanks. Sometimes I play what I call the "thanks game" with another brother or sister for this purpose. For several minutes we take turns thanking God for specific blessings. This is difficult to begin with, but it is surprisingly helpful!

- I express thanks to other people for small kindnesses as well as big favors. I find that this breaks down my pride, builds other people up, and promotes genuine unity. I am not as consistent at this as I'd like to be, but I've made some progress by God's grace.

- I read quality books on biblical thankfulness, like the ones I've quoted in this chapter. This help me focus deeply on thankfulness, it deepens my convictions about it, and it provides many practical suggestions.

Cultivating thanksgiving is deeply counter-intuitive to our fallen human hearts. But it is an expression of faith in God that delights Him and unleashes His power to transform us!

Chapter 12
Colossians 3:12-16
The Path to Spiritual Maturity – Part #4

Embracing a Lifestyle of Love: Building Unity with Other Christians

As we have seen in the last few chapters, Paul's instruction on how to grow to spiritual maturity consists of two main parts. Foundationally, we need to cultivate a mental focus on what God has provided for us through Christ (Colossians 3:1-4). Then we need to embrace a lifestyle consistent with what God has provided for you through Christ (Colossians 3:5-17). This involves putting aside a lifestyle of self-centeredness and putting on a lifestyle of biblical love. This loving lifestyle has three relational foci: God, one another, and people who don't know Christ. In this chapter we will look more closely at the second focus: loving other Christians.

> ^{3:12} So, as those who have been chosen of God, holy and beloved, put on a heart of compassion, kindness, humility, gentleness and patience; ¹³ bearing with *one another*, and forgiving *each other*, whoever has a complaint against anyone; just as the Lord forgave you, so also should you. ¹⁴ Beyond all these things put on love, which is the perfect bond of unity. ¹⁵ Let the peace of Christ rule in your hearts, to which indeed you were called in one body; and be thankful. ¹⁶ Let the word of Christ richly dwell within you, with all wisdom teaching and admonishing *one another* with psalms and hymns and spiritual songs, singing with thankfulness in your hearts to God.

You can see by Paul's usage of "one another" and "each other" (3:13,16) that he is referring to Christians relating to other Christians. In this case, "put on love" is connected to "unity" between Christians (3:14). Likewise, "the peace of Christ" (3:15) is here a synonym for sociological unity between Christians, not psychological peace within Christians (as in Philippians 4:7). So Paul is teaching that embracing a lifestyle of love involves building unity with other Christians. Let's ask the same three questions about unity that we asked in the last chapter about thankfulness: What is this unity? Why is unity so important? How can we build unity?

What is this unity?

The New Testament speaks of different kinds of unity between Christians, so it's important to understand which kind of unity is in view here.

- There is *collaboration* unity between churches—as when different Christian churches work together functionally on a project. Paul called his Gentile churches to collaborate in giving money to help their Jewish brethren in Jerusalem (see 1 Corinthians 16:1-4; 2 Corinthians 8,9). Our church collaborates with many other churches and ministries on many different projects. But Paul makes no reference to this kind of unity in this passage.

- There is also *organizational* unity within a local church— creating and maintaining structures and other policies that enable a church to function in an orderly way. Paul reminds Timothy and Titus of the need for organizational unity in his letters to him (see 1 Timothy 3:5; Titus 1:5ff.). Our church has developed these structures and policies over the years, and they are very important. But this kind of unity is not in view here—Paul makes no reference to it, either.

- The unity in view here is *personal, relational* unity between Christians in the same local church. Because the local church is the family of God, it should prioritize developing a strong network of Christ-centered friendships among its members. This unity is foundational, which is why the New Testament speaks far more about it than the other kinds of unity. It is the context in which Christians can mature spiritually, and it enables the other two kinds of unity to develop in healthy ways. All too often, contemporary western churches focus on collaboration unity or organizational unity while neglecting relational unity. The cost of this neglect is huge, as we will see.

Why is this unity so important?

Why does every single New Testament letter emphasize this kind of unity, while only a few passages talk about the other kinds of unity?

- *Effective evangelism is impossible without it.* Earlier, we noted what Jesus taught His disciples about the importance of this kind of unity.

John 13:34 "A new commandment I give to you, that you love one another, even as I have loved you, that you also love one another. ³⁵ "By this all men will know that you are My disciples, if you have love for one another."

Notice that Jesus doesn't call this "one of many options;" He calls it His "commandment" (mandate) to us. What does it take to convince people that Jesus is a living Person whose leadership can change people's lives? Of course, we need to share the gospel with them and give them reasons why we know it is true. Of course, we need to share how Jesus has personally changed our lives. But this verbal sharing *must* be accompanied by observable love between Christians—the same kind of love that Jesus showed the disciples—if it is to be persuasive. Just as the lyrics of a song often get our attention only after the melody has drawn us in, so the message of Christianity often gets people's attention only after this loving unity has aroused our curiosity and interest.

"God's plan is that local bodies of believing Christians... (become) a dynamic community in which (evangelism) becomes intensely productive. The church that convinces people that there is a God is a church that manifests what only a God can do, that is, to unite human beings in love... There is nothing that convinces people that God exists or that awakens their craving for Him like the discovery of Christian brothers and sisters who love one another... The sight of loving unity among Christians arrests the non-Christian. It crashes through his intellect, stirs up his conscience and creates a tumult of longing in his heart because he was created to enjoy the very thing that you are demonstrating."[1]

The numerical decline of true Christians in America is a well-documented fact. Devout Christians rightly lament this fact, and promote many evangelistic media projects, training programs and strategies in the hope of arresting this decline. Some of these efforts are very good, some are not so good, and some are counter-productive. But even the best of them will never turn the tide. We will never be able to out-market or out-entertain our culture. We have two things that our culture does not have—the message of God's grace and real loving unity—and God designed them to go *together.* Doctrinal fidelity to God's grace will not get the job done without demonstrating this loving unity.

- *Spiritual maturity is impossible without it.* Spiritual maturity is increasing in Christ-like character, which Paul elsewhere calls the "fruit of the Spirit" (Galatians 5:22,23). Which context is more likely to develop good character in

---

[1] John White, *The Fight* (InterVarsity Press, 1979), pp. 149,150.

children—24/7 day-care centers, or family life? Character
requires nurture, modeling, personalized instruction, loving
discipline, appropriate responsibilities, supervision, etc.—
and this is what a loving family can best provide.

Some of us have had the good fortune of growing up in healthy
families. Many of us did not have this opportunity, and our
character-development has suffered as a result. But thank God that
He has provided us with a new family in which we can develop
Christ-like character! That family is called "the local church," and
that healthy, character-developing family life is called "unity." But if
the local church is to develop maturing members, *each* of us must
make building unity a high practical priority—much higher, for
example, than entertainment and career advancement. No wonder
virtually every New Testament letter contains a passage like this one!

How can we build this unity?

Paul gives us two key steps to build this unity. The Bible describes
other key steps, but these two are foundational.

First, we can *help one other be filled with the Word of Christ.*

> [3,16] Let the word of Christ richly dwell within you, with all
> wisdom teaching and admonishing one another; with
> psalms and hymns and spiritual songs, singing with
> thankfulness in your hearts to God.

We covered this verse several chapters ago when we studied 1:9-12
and 1:28,29, so we will just review it briefly. "The Word of Christ"
refers especially to "the things above"—all that God has freely given
us through Christ. It also refers to rejecting a self-centered way of
life and embracing a lifestyle of love. We should not live on a
subsistence intake of the Word of Christ. God wants it to "richly
dwell within us"—to be so at home in us that it increasingly
dominates our thinking and our decisions.

Paul says that being indwelt by the Word of Christ involves communicating it to "one another." This means that we cannot be filled by the Word of Christ in isolation. No amount of private reading and study can take the place of regularly sharing Christ's Word with other Christians by teaching (reading, explaining, reminding) one another, admonishing (counseling, warning, correcting) one another, and praying out loud (including thanking God) with one another.

Large meetings play an important role in our Christian lives, but they are not conducive to communicating the Word of Christ to one another. This requires initiating and maintaining a network of Christ-centered friendships. Such friendships flourish best by being committed to a home group that emphasizes through-the-week personal discipleship relationships. These relationships form the very heart of true Christian unity!

What step in this direction is God putting before you? Is it to investigate a home group? Is it to commit to a home group? Is it to ask someone in your home group about getting together regularly to practice Colossians 3:16? God always gives us a doable step in this direction. And when we take it, we will be building the unity that please Him and helps us toward spiritual maturity!

Second, we can *persevere with one another despite our messiness and sinfulness.*

> 3:12 So, as those who have been chosen of God, holy and beloved, put on a heart of compassion, kindness, humility, gentleness and patience; 13 bearing with one another, and forgiving each other, whoever has a complaint against anyone; just as the Lord forgave you, so also should you.

If you get involved in the kind of Christ-centered friendships described above, you will need to work diligently to build and maintain real unity in these friendships (see Ephesians 4:2,3). Paul is totally realistic here in his description of Christian unity. What kind of people need compassion, kindness, humility, gentleness, patience, forbearance, and forgiveness? Really broken people, people who have really messy lives, people who still have lots of sin! That's the kind of person you and I are—there are no other kinds of Christians. For this reason, we need to commit ourselves to one another for the long haul, and we need to love each other in ways that don't come naturally to us.

- We need to express *compassion*—empathy for one another's suffering—rather than being cold and insensitive.

- We need to express *kindness*—actively blessing one another—rather than being relationally passive or demanding.

- We need to express *gentleness*—strength under self-control in order to help—rather than run over one another with the truth.

- We need to express *patience*—literally "slow to anger"— rather than blowing up or "moving on" when things get difficult.

- We need to *bear with one another*, rather than withdraw because we're fed up with one another's idiosyncrasies and besetting sins.

- We need to *forgive* one another when others sin against us, instead of paying them back or rejecting them.

- Undergirding all these character qualities, we need *humility*—an other-centered servant attitude—rather than being boastful or self-absorbed, or demanding our rights, or deciding "I didn't sign up for this!"

These character qualities form an index of our involvement with other Christians. Are you involved enough with some Christian friends that you need to bear with their annoying idiosyncrasies and besetting sins? Are you involved enough that you need to extend forgiveness when they disappoint or offend you? Are you involved enough that you need to express compassion even though you can't personally relate to their current sufferings? If you can't answer "Yes" to these questions, you're not involved enough!

How do we get the motivation to build and maintain this kind of unity? It can't come primarily from the perks we get when other brothers and sisters love us well! It comes rather from remembering and focusing on the fact that this is the way God loves us.

> 3:12 So, *as those who have been chosen of God, holy and beloved,* put on a heart of compassion, kindness, humility, gentleness and patience; 13 bearing with one another, and forgiving each other, whoever has a complaint against anyone; *just as the Lord forgave you,* so also should you.

Personalize what Paul says in 3:13: "Even though I deserved Your judgment, You forgave me at the cost of Your own Son's death. On that same basis, You continue to forgive me and bear with all of my weird idiosyncrasies and besetting sins. In view of this, how can I not extend forgiveness and forbearance to my Christian friends?"

Personalize what Paul says in 3:12: "While I was still rebelling against You, You humbly took the initiative toward me, and set me apart as Your child. Even though I am still full of sin and folly, You continue to pour out Your compassion and kindness and gentleness and patience on me. In view of this, how can I not extend compassion and kindness and gentleness and patience to my Christian friends?"

The key to building unity in this way, then, is not how messy your Christian friends' lives get, or how badly they treat you. It is whether you let their messiness and sins deepen your appreciation of God's love for you in spite of your own messiness and sin!

What Christian friend is God asking you to persevere with? What expression of persevering love is He asking you to express to them? How is He showing you that He loves you in this same way? God loves to answer these questions if we ask Him!

Chapter 13
Colossians 3:17
The Path to Spiritual Maturity — Part #5

Representing Jesus in Our Social Roles

^{3:17} Whatever you do in word or deed, do all in the name of the Lord Jesus, giving thanks through Him to God the Father.

A transitional verse

Colossians 3:17 is a "pivot" verse; it both looks back to what Paul has just taught, and introduces what he is about to teach. Paul has been teaching about the importance of love relationships in authentic Christian spirituality. To this end, he has urged us to love God by cultivating a thankful prayer life (3:15b,16b). He has also urged us to love other Christians in ways that build true unity (3:12-16).

Now Paul applies this same emphasis on loving to how we relate to people within our various social roles, many of whom may not believe in Christ. Paul speaks here of our spouses (3:18,19), our parents and children (3:20,21), and those at our work-places (3:22-4:1). In other passages also he speaks of governing authorities (Romans 13:1-7) and neighbors (Romans 13:9,10) and fellow-citizens (Titus 3:1,2).

Colossians 3:17 is an over-arching principle that should govern all of these relationships. It is important, therefore, that we understand what this principle means before we look at Paul's specific teaching on our social roles.

What does this principle mean?

The heart of this principle is: "Do all in the name of the Lord Jesus." The NLT helpfully translates this phrase: "Do it as a representative of the Lord Jesus." To do something in someone's name means to act is that person's representative. An American ambassador is in fact a representative of the President, so he should speak and acts in ways that accurately represent the President and his policies. This principle calls us to remember that we are Jesus' representatives before the watching world, and to live in a way that accurately and attractively represents Him.

Furthermore, Paul urges us to give thanks to Jesus as we represent Him to the watching world. This may mean that we should thank Jesus for the privilege of being His representatives in all of these social roles. Not only does Jesus forgive our sins and make us God's children; He also allows us to be His ambassadors at home and at work and in our neighborhoods and in every place! Our thankfulness to Jesus is also a key way in which we represent Jesus to others. This doesn't mean that we literally say "Thank You Jesus" every time we interact with people. Rather, it means that a thankful attitude toward Jesus should govern our interactions with others, rather than a self-centered, entitled attitude—which leads to grumbling and disputing with others (Philippians 2:14,15).

Finally, notice the scope of this principle: "Whatever you do, in word or in deed." We should seek to represent Jesus accurately through our conduct all of our social roles (on which Paul elaborates in Colossians 3:18-4:1). We should also seek to represent Jesus well through our words (on which Paul elaborates in Colossians 4:2-6). We will explore this rich passage in the next four chapters.

Why is our conduct so important?

Most of Paul's letters to his churches contain instructions on conduct that represents Jesus in our social roles.[1] He also urges Timothy and Titus to instruct their churches on this subject.[2] Peter gives this same instruction in one of his letters.[3] From this repetition we learn that representing Jesus through our conduct toward non-Christians is vitally important and integrally related to representing Him through our speech. This does not mean that our conduct *is* evangelism. "Evangelism" means "communicating the gospel," and the gospel is a verbal message that must be communicated through words. People receive salvation by believing this message, not by being impressed by our conduct. Nor does it mean that we must first demonstrate godly conduct to people before we share the gospel with them. The Bible narrates many Christians who share the gospel with strangers. But most of our evangelism will be with people with whom we regularly interact through our social roles. And our conduct in these relationships is crucially important because it has the power to make our message more or less credible. Our conduct can "adorn" the gospel, making it attractive (Titus 2:10), or it can give people an excuse to dishonor this message (Titus 2:5).

In the following chapters, we will consider how this principle applies to our family and work roles. In the remainder of this chapter, we will consider some additional biblical truths that bear on this subject.

---

[1] See Romans 12:17-13:17; 1 Corinthians 6:1-8; Ephesians 5:22-6:9; Philippians 2:14-18; Colossians 3:18-4:1.

[2] See 1 Timothy 6:1,2; Titus 2:9-3:2.

[3] See 1 Peter 2:11-3:9.

Christian community and representing Jesus in our social roles

Whenever New Testament letters teach on our social roles, the authors' usually precede this instruction with instruction about the importance of Christian community. This is exactly what Paul did in Colossians 3:12-16. We may infer from this that *involvement in Christian community is necessary to represent Jesus well in our social roles.*

Why do so many Christians fail at being Christ-honoring spouses or parents or work-associates or citizens? Western Christians often point to deficiencies like laziness, poor time-management, dishonesty, grouchiness, and disrespect. All of these adversely affect our witness for Christ. But western Christians seldom criticize superficial or sporadic engagement with other Christians. This is a blind spot that is costing Christ's reputation! Only by prioritizing Christ-centered friendships will we have the necessary spiritual encouragement and nourishment to represent Jesus well in our social roles. Only by praying regularly with our Christian friends will we call down God's power to create opportunities for witness in our social roles. Only by enjoying the goodness of Christ-centered friendships we will be protected from the cynicism and seductive temptations we face in our social roles.

Western Christian leaders rightly lament the increasing godlessness of our nations. Many of them seek to reverse this development by urging Christians to secure positions of influence and decision-making power in education, the market-place, government, and entertainment. One problem with this strategy is that the New Testament does not prescribe it. True, God sometimes sovereignly moves His people into such roles. He did this with Daniel in the Old Testament. We read in the New Testament of people who became Christians while already in these roles—like Erastus the city treasurer of Corinth (Acts 19:22; Romans 16:23). God has continued to do this throughout the history of the church. For example, God worked through William Wilberforce as a member of British Parliament to abolish the British slave trade. But we do not find one verse that urges Christians to get into these roles.[4] One reason for this may be that Christians who pursue this strategy must usually pay the price of isolation from Christian fellowship. This often leads to ineffectiveness or even compromise in their witness for Christ. We should return to the New Testament's primary strategy for influencing our society. Instead of urging Christians to get into powerful social roles, we should urge one another to represent Jesus well in whatever social roles we occupy. And we should urge one another to invest deeply in Christian community so we can be spiritually potent in our social roles.

Human authority structures and representing Jesus in our social roles

Representing Jesus in our social roles involves responding properly to the authority structures in which these roles operate. Paul upholds the basic legitimacy of human authority in the home and workplace and civil government. As we will see in the following chapters, Colossians 3:18–4:1 calls Christian wives to submit to their husbands, Christian children to submit to their parents, and Christian slaves to submit to their masters. Other passages call Christians to submit to their governing authorities (see 1 Peter 2:13,14) and to church authorities (see Hebrews 13:17). These same passages implicitly affirm the legitimacy of these offices of authority. Otherwise, the Bible would never call us to submit to them. God established them to preserve order and deter evil in a deeply broken and fallen world (see Romans 13:1–4). We dismiss the importance of

---

[4] To say that the New Testament authors don't command this because few Christians had opportunity to secure such roles is an argument from silence.

human authority to our own peril! That is why Paul never calls for its abolition.

Some Christians conclude from the above that we should be social conservatives who preserve the status quo in traditional societies. But this is a mistake. God's kingdom has broken into this fallen world through Jesus' coming and the creation of His Body, the church. As Christians, we should not abolish the world's social structures, but rather relate to them in new ways in light of our relationships with Jesus. This is why the New Testament authors stand out in stark contrast to the conservative Greek, Roman and Jewish social teaching of their day.[5] For example:

- *Our identity is independent of our social roles.* The assumption of Paul's contemporary conservative teachers was that "one's identity is determined by one's social role." In other words, husbands, masters and rulers were intrinsically superior—while wives, workers and subjects were intrinsically inferior. This is the essence of chauvinism. So Jewish historian Josephus says, "A woman is inferior to her husband in all things. Let her, *therefore,* be obedient to him... "[6] Greco-Roman moral philosophers called women by such names as "worthless," "silly," and "innately inferior to men."[7] Jewish rabbi Philo also taught that wives were to "serve as slaves" to their husbands, and that "the only purpose of marriage was procreation."[8] They referred to slaves as: "a thing," "a mortal object," "chattel,"

---

[5] For examples, see Attalus of Pergamum (as recorded in Polybius, *Histories* 18.41.8-9), Philo (*DeDecalago* 165-167), Josephus (*Against Apion* II.25-30), and the Stoic thinkers Epictetus, Diogenes Laertius, and Pseudo-Phocylides.

[6] Flavius Josephus, *Against Apion* II. 25 (Kregel Publications, 1981), p. 632.

[7] Cited in Richard N. Longenecker, *New Testament Social Ethics for Today* (Eerdmans Publishing, 1984), pp. 71,72.

[8] Richard N. Longenecker, *New Testament Social Ethics for Today*, p. 73.

and "tools with breath."[9] Jewish rabbis prayed, "Blessed be He that He did not make me a Gentile; blessed be He that He did not make me a boor (slave); blessed be He that He did not make me a woman."[10] Greeks thanked the gods "...that I was born a human being and not a beast, next, a man and not a woman, thirdly, a Greek and not a barbarian."[11]

How different Paul's perspective is! As we saw in Colossians 3:10,11, he taught that human identity is established by being created in God's image and is therefore independent of our social roles. Furthermore, all believers have a new identity in Christ as brothers and sisters in God's family. Our different genders and social roles, while not obliterated, are now overshadowed by our fundamental equality in Christ.

Galatians 3:28 There is neither Jew nor Greek, there is neither slave nor free man, there is neither male nor female; for you are all one in Christ Jesus.

This perspective was unheard of in the ancient world! Modern western assumptions about human equality and human rights come from biblical passages like this one.

- *Obedience to human authorities is conditional.* Traditional social systems often gave to human authorities ultimate power over their subjects. In contrast, the Bible clearly teaches that all human authority is subject to God's authority, and that therefore all human authority is limited.

---

[9] Richard N. Longenecker, *New Testament Social Ethics for Today*, p. 49.

[10] Credited to Rabbi Judah b. Elai (c. AD 150) in *Tos Berakoth* 7:18 and *Jer Berakoth* 13b, and to Rabbi Meier (c. AD 150) in *Bab Menahoth* 43b.

[11] Attributed to Thales and Socrates in Diogenes Laertius' *Vitae Philosophorum* 1.33, to Plato in Plutarch's *Marius* 46.1 and in Lactantius' *Divine Institutes* 3.19.17.

If human authorities command us to disobey God, or if they forbid us to do what God commands, we must respectfully disobey them in order to obey God (see Daniel 3:16-18; Acts 4:19,20; 5:19).

Submission, which the New Testament authors call us to express to all human authorities, is not the same as obedience. Submission is an attitude of respect for the office-holder, and a willingness to facilitate their legitimate goals. We can therefore be submissive even when we must disobey!

Likewise, human authority is valid only within its proper, God-ordained spheres. Husbands have authority over their own wives, not over women in general. Parents have authority over their own children, not over other children. Employers have authority over their employees at work, not outside of the work-place. Governing officials have authority over citizens with regard to civic matters like traffic laws, not over their religious or philosophical beliefs. Granted, these areas often overlap, and drawing clear lines between these spheres can be difficult. But this principle is very different from traditional chauvinistic social systems.

- *Our primary motivation for playing our social roles is to serve God rather than to serve ourselves or other people.* Richard Longenecker's summary of what motivated slaves is representative for all subordinate social roles in traditional societies: "Slavery was an oppressive thing for most, shot through with fear, malice, and resentment."[12] In other words, "Go along where you must, in order to stay out of

---

[12] Richard N. Longenecker, *New Testament Social Ethics for Today,* p. 49.

trouble and protect your limited freedoms as much as possible."

How different is the motivation that Paul emphasizes! When we play subordinate roles, we should voluntarily pursue the authorities' legitimate goals as a way of serving Christ (Colossians 3:23 – "Do your work heartily, as for the Lord;" Colossians 3:24 – "It is the Lord Christ you serve"). And God will reward us for this service to Him, regardless of how they treat us (Colossians 3:24 – "from the Lord you will receive the reward of the inheritance"). This motivation gives great dignity to our social roles and should lead to excellence in attitude and behavior, as we will see in the next few chapters.

Eduard Schweizer summarizes how most ancient social thinkers instructed those in positions of authority: "The aim... is the self-protection (and detachment) of the male, adult and free man, who, in order to reach... (his own inner harmony) should remember the right attitude towards inferiors..."[13] This mentality is still very much with us: "I've got to manage my wife, kids, and employees so they don't get in my way, so I can do what I want."

How different is the motivation that Paul emphasizes! When we are in authority roles, we should follow Jesus' example by using our authority to serve those under our charge (Colossians 4:1 – "Masters, grant to your slaves justice and fairness"). And we should remember that we are under Christ's authority and will give an account to Him

---

[13] Eduard Schweizer, "Traditional Ethical Patterns in the Pauline and Post-Pauline Letters and Their Development," *Text and Interpretation*, ed. E. Best and R. M. Wilson (Cambridge University Press, 1979), p. 202.

for how we played this role (Colossians 4:1 – "...knowing that you too have a Master in heaven").

As we move forward

Keep this big picture in mind as we study Paul's teaching about specific social roles in Colossians 3:18–4:1. This will help you to avoid misunderstanding Paul as a social conservative or a social revolutionary, so that he can equip you to play your social roles as Jesus' representative.

Chapter 14
Colossians 3:18,19
The Path to Spiritual Maturity — Part #6

A Biblical Framework for Marriage

In this chapter, we will look at a biblical framework for marriage. Paul provides us with a greatly distilled version of this framework.

> [3.18] Wives, be subject to your husbands, as is fitting in the Lord. [19] Husbands, love your wives and do not be embittered against them.

Drawing upon additional biblical passages, we will look first at the structure of marriage, and then consider some key guidelines for a healthy marriage relationship. For those of you who are unmarried, this material is important for at least two reasons. First, in the event that you get married, you need to know what you're getting into! Second, some of these biblical guidelines for healthy marriage relationships also apply to other close relationships.

Authority and roles in marriage

As we saw in the previous chapter, the Bible teaches that God has created offices of human authority. He does this primarily to restrain evil and provide social order in a world where people are now inclined to do their own will rather than follow His will. God is very realistic about human authority—He knows that it can be abused and He condemns that abuse, but He says that in this age imperfect human authority is preferable to no structure at all. This is the case in marriage as well as our other social roles, even though there are significant differences in the way each of these offices function.

Paul affirms this structure within marriage by reminding the wives in the Colossian church to "be subject to your husbands, as is fitting in the Lord." God has given Christian husbands the responsibility and authority to lead in their marriages.[1] What does this look like in a biblical marriage? Contrary to what you may have heard, it looks nothing like male chauvinism! The qualifications the Bible puts on this structure reject, rather than support, male chauvinism.

- *Husbands are not superior to wives.* Rejecting the consensus of its day, the Bible teaches that men and women are equal in their essential identity as image-bearers of God (Genesis 1:27; Colossians 3:10,11). This means that our social roles do not create or affect our identities. The fact that a husband plays a certain role in marriage doesn't make him superior to his wife any more than a policeman is superior to other citizens.

- *Women should not be subject to all men.* The call to be subject is always limited (as it is in this passage) to "your own husbands." This means that women are under no obligation to men in general. This also implies that women

---

[1]Many contemporary evangelicals reject this teaching, perhaps because of how it has been used to justify male chauvinism. But several passages (like this one) affirm this basic structure, and the attempts to reinterpret these passages in strictly egalitarian ways are invalid. Some say that male headship in marriage was merely an accommodation to the culture, and that since our culture no longer affirms male headship we are free to reject it. But Paul's parallel of the husband and wife to Christ and the church (Ephesians 5:23–25) indicate that this relationship transcends cultural norms. Some say that "head" (Ephesians 5:23) means "source" (as in a river source), so that Paul is merely calling on husbands to be the source of love for their wives— not to provide leadership. Of course, husbands are to love their wives, as Colossians 3:19 says. But the context of these passages (i.e., leadership responsibility for parents, employers, and governing authorities) makes it clear that an office of authority is also in view, even though there are significant differences in the way each of these offices function. Furthermore, to say that husbands should be the source of love for their wives is both unbiblical and demeaning to women, because Christ is the Source of love for both husbands and wives.

should have equal opportunity for advancement in the workplace.

- *Wives should correct their husbands when needed.* While affirming the authority structure, Paul insists on mutual subjection to Christ within the marriage relationship. Paul states this explicitly in Ephesians 5:21 when he calls all Christians to "be subject to *one another* in the fear of Christ." This is not a one-way street; Christian husbands should also receive appropriate biblical instruction and admonition from their wives.

- *Wives should not unconditionally obey their husbands, or submit to abusive treatment.* The Bible clearly teaches that all human authority is subject to God's authority, and that therefore when human authority commands us to disobey God, we must respectfully disobey human authority (see Daniel 3:18; 6:10; Acts 4:19,20; 5:19). Wives also have recourse to other authorities, including the local church and the police, to intervene should their husbands' behavior be abusive.

- *Wives should not necessarily limit their activity to the home.* The Bible holds child-rearing in very high regard and opposes the current sentiment that women who choose to quit their careers to focus full-time on their children are second-class citizens. But it also affirms wives as active workers and leaders in the church (see Romans 16:1-3) and in the work world (see Proverbs 31:16,24).

- *Husbands should not use their authority to get what they want.* Jesus specifically forbade this abuse of authority in Mark 10:42-45, and called all of His followers to follow His example by using their authority to sacrificially serve others.

> Mark 10:[42] "You know that those who are recognized as rulers of the Gentiles lord it over them; and their great men exercise authority over them. [43] But it is not this way among you, but whoever wishes to become great among you shall be your servant; [44] and whoever wishes to be first among you shall be slave of all. [45] For even the Son of Man did not come to be served, but to serve, and to give His life a ransom for many."

Paul likewise specifically calls on husbands to imitate Jesus by using their authority to sacrificially serve their wives.

> Ephesians 5:[25] Husbands, love your wives, just as Christ also loved the church and gave Himself up for her...

Headship in marriage, then, is not a license for selfish advantage; it is responsibility to initiate sacrificial, serving love.

Therefore, those who blame the Bible for male chauvinism (and those who claim the Bible supports their male chauvinism) have either never studied it carefully, or have willfully distorted its teaching. The truth about the biblical view's historical effect on society is actually just the opposite, as Francis Schaeffer points out:

"In a fallen world it is not surprising to see that men have turned this structure into a kind of slavery. It is not meant to be a slavery. In fact, it is in cultures where the Bible has been influential that the balance (between structure and love) has been substantially restored."[2]

When should a husband exercise this decision-making authority? Christian scholars and pastors answer this question in different ways. Here is my conclusion: *In major decisions not clearly addressed in scripture, if after careful and prayerful discussion*

---

[2] Francis A. Schaeffer, *Genesis in Space and Time* (InterVarsity Press, 1972), p. 94.

husband and wife cannot agree, the husband should assume the
responsibility to make the decision that he thinks will best advance
God's glory and the family's good. Let's consider this principle
phrase by phrase.

- "In major decisions not clearly addressed in scripture..." In
  those decisions that are clearly addressed in scripture,
  husband and wife should mutually submit to what God
  says. In less important decisions, husbands should not say:
  "I'm in authority, so I get what I want!" Nor should
  husbands or wives say: "You got your way last time; it's my
  turn!" Instead, both spouses should be ready to defer in love
  to the other spouses' preference. How wonderful it is to see
  spouses "fighting" in this way!

- "...if after careful and prayerful discussion..." Sometimes my
  wife persuades me that the course she advocates is better.
  God sometimes convicts me that my motives for my course
  are selfish. Sometimes my wife is persuaded or convicted in
  a similar way. When both of us humbly seek the Lord's will
  together in this way, we almost always eventually come to a
  common conviction.

- "...the husband should assume the responsibility..." This
  authority is not a privilege; it is a sober responsibility.
  Husbands will answer to God for the decisions they make
  concerning their marriages and families, so they should
  take their decision-making stewardship very seriously and
  prayerfully. This includes asking counsel from others.

- "...to make the decision that he thinks will best advance
  God's glory and the family's good." The basis for the
  decision should never be what I like best or what is to my
  immediate advantage. In a Christ-centered marriage,
  husbands rarely need to exercise this authority. But it is

there for those cases when it is needed. The resolution then
is not to vote or to take turns on getting what you want—
but to move forward in this way. And in these cases, God
calls on wives to respect their husbands' office and
cooperate with a good attitude.

While this principle may not answer all your questions, it provides a
biblical framework within which you can seek God's personal
guidance. Often, His guidance comes through the counsel of solid
Christians—especially those who know you well. This is one reason
why Paul precedes his instruction to spouses with an exhortation to
be deeply involved in Christian community (see Colossians 3:12-16).
Christian marriages do not thrive in isolation from other Christians;
they thrive with the ongoing love and support and wisdom that only
other Christians can supply.

Guidelines for a healthy marriage relationship

Paul distills his instruction to Christian husbands to "love your wives
and do not be embittered against them." *Pikraino* can also be
translated "be harsh with" – and the ESV, NIV, and NLT all prefer this
translation. Paul seems to be warning husbands against a harsh,
authoritarian attitude and urging them to cherish and nurture their
wives as treat themselves. Certainly this is his emphasis in his
parallel letter, Ephesians:

> Ephesians 5:[25] Husbands, love your wives, just as Christ also
> loved the church and gave Himself up for her [26] so that He
> might sanctify her, having cleansed her by the washing of
> water with the word, [27] that He might present to Himself the
> church in all her glory, having no spot or wrinkle or any
> such thing; but that she would be holy and blameless. [28] So
> husbands ought also to love their own wives as their own
> bodies. He who loves his own wife loves himself.

Of course, both husbands and wives should love one another. What kind of loving relating characterizes healthy Christian marriages?

- *Communicate respect to your spouse.* Peter urges Christian husbands to "show (your wives) honor as a fellow heir in the grace of life" (1 Peter 3:7b). This applies to both husbands and wives! How sad it is to see spouses erode their relationship by being cold, dismissive, speaking harshly, and treating each other with contempt! Conversely, when spouses consistently communicate respect to one another, they form a foundation for a God-glorifying and satisfying marriage. Consider the following questions, which probe this area of marriage:

Do you express appreciation for your spouse's good qualities—both directly to him or her, and to others? We often lose sight of these good qualities, giving more attention to our spouses' annoying idiosyncrasies and besetting sins. Even when we see these good qualities, we can be reluctant to acknowledge them because of competitive pride.

Do you ask your spouse for advice? Few things communicate genuine respect like asking for input on major decisions, ministry situations, and personal struggles. Besides, our spouses are often best suited to give us valuable advice because they know us so well.

Do you receive correction from your spouse? Sadly, this key aspect of biblical love is absent from most marriages. It is easy to buy into the prideful lie that if you receive correction, you will lose respect (though nothing could be further from the truth in most cases). We avoid the conflict that correction may cause. We deflect corrective input by changing the subject or being defensive. We teach our spouses not to correct us by erupting in anger or giving them the silent treatment. But when we listen carefully, and thank them for their input, and carefully consider it, and acknowledge what is true,

we communicate respect to our spouses and grow in our own
personal maturity.

- *Prioritize positive emotional investment.* The command to
  love one another includes expressing our love in ways that
  help our spouses *feel* loved. Gary Chapman emphasizes this
  priority through his instruction on "love languages."[3] We
  experience love emotionally on different "frequencies:"
  giving undivided attention, speaking caring words, giving
  unexpected gifts, initiating helpful deeds, giving
  appropriate physical touch, etc. Husbands and wives rarely
  "speak" the same love languages. Because of our self-
  centeredness, we naturally tend to express love emotionally
  to our spouses in the ways that make *us* feel loved. This is
  why a husband may feel unloved by his physically
  unaffectionate wife—but she protests and cites all the
  practical ways she serves him. This is why a wife may feel
  unloved by her sexually interested husband who rarely
  inquires about what's happening in her life and how she
  feels about it.

  This was a real revelation to me! It explained why my wife
  didn't feel loved when I asked her to split wood with me! It
  also explained her response when I called her from work
  (for the first time in seven years of marriage) to ask how
  her day was going. Imagine my surprise when she finally
  asked: "Who is this?"

  When we learn our spouses' love languages, and then find
  ways to communicate love on those "frequencies" (even
  when they feel uncomfortable for us), our marriages
  usually begin to flourish. A backlog of positive emotional
  investment begins to accumulate, and this backlog acts as a

---

[3] Gary Chapman, "Toward a Growing Marriage: A Biblical Seminar on Marriage," Lecture #4.

buffer from day to day irritants and idiosyncrasies. Yes, we need to resist hurtful language and apologize when we use it. Yes, we need to talk out conflicts as they come up. But consistent positive emotional investment is what builds mutual appreciation and makes forgiveness and forbearance easier to extend.

- *Focus more on becoming a better spouse than on making your spouse better.* Our text says: "Be subject to your spouse... and love your spouse." Yet we tend to pervert this into a demand on our spouses: "Be sure that your spouse is subject to you... (and) loves you." This love-demanding focus promotes frustration, anxiety, manipulation, guilt motivation, and other counter-productive marital habits. But when we entrust our spouses into God's hands and focus on cooperating with how He wants to change us, good things happen. We begin to experience the peace that comes from embracing His will. We experience increasing freedom from frustration with our spouses. And ironically, we exert more influence for godly change in them! Peter's advice in this regard to wives applies equally to husbands:

1 Peter 3:[1] In the same way, you wives, be submissive to your own husbands so that even if any of them are disobedient to the word, they may be won without a word by the behavior of their wives, [2] as they observe your chaste and respectful behavior. [3] Your adornment must not be merely external... [4] but let it be the hidden person of the heart, with the imperishable quality of a gentle and quiet spirit, which is precious in the sight of God.

- *Look to Christ to meet your deepest needs instead of to your spouse.* Love is not primarily a feeling; it is a choice to serve sacrificially (even when it is costly for us to do so) and freely (without expectation of return). The problem is that we are very needy people, and because of our fallennness, we often look to our spouses rather than to God to meet our deepest needs.

I enjoy the beautiful vows couples make at their weddings. But on some level I know they are actually thinking something very different. The bride may vow to stand by her husband no matter what, but she is probably thinking: "You make me feel secure, and I'm counting on you to do this for me for the rest of my life." The groom may vow to cherish his wife from this day forward, but he is probably thinking: "You make feel so important and significant, and I'm counting on you to do this for me for the rest of my life."

These expectations place a burden on our spouses that they cannot bear. This is one of the most frequent reason for marital failure. And this is why the number one requirement for a successful marriage is spiritual—that we learn how to depend on God to meet these needs.

What Paul teaches in Colossians about Christ and His provision for us is the foundation for a good marriage, just as it is the foundation for every other relationship in our lives. This is why after we receive Christ, we need to cultivate a mindset focused on what He has given us, and trust Him to enable us to give His love to others. Then we can be grateful givers, and we can serve freely.

Chapter 15
Colossians 3:20,21
The Path to Spiritual Maturity — Part #7

A Biblical Framework for Parenting

In this chapter, we will look at a biblical framework for parenting. As with marriage in the previous two verses, Paul provides us with a very concise overview of this framework.

> [3, 20] Children, be obedient to your parents in all things, for this is well-pleasing to the Lord. [21] Fathers, do not exasperate your children, so that they will not lose heart.

"Fathers" (*pateres*) here probably refers collectively to both parents.[1] "Children" (*techna*) refers to younger children, still under their parents' direct care—not adult children. Since Epaphras had probably instructed the Colossian Christians on this subject in more depth, Paul summarizes that instruction. He provides another, slightly different summary in a parallel passage:

Ephesians 6: [1] Children, obey your parents in the Lord, for this is right. [2] Honor your father and mother (which is the first commandment with a promise), [3] so that it may be well with you, and that you may live long on the earth. [4] Fathers, do not provoke your children to anger, but bring them up in the discipline (training) and instruction (correction) of the Lord.

---

[1] See this usage in Hebrews 11:23.

Parenting is a vast and complex subject. But by examining these two passages and drawing upon other biblical passages, we can distill three inter-related priorities in Christian parenting: positive love investment, corrective discipline, and spiritual development. For each priority, we will consider realistic goals and practical steps to help accomplish those goals. As we do this, we will see our need for God's wisdom and power to become more godly parents.

Positive love investment

Parents and children are made in God's image, which means that (above all else) we are persons who can relate in love to other persons. The heart of the parent-child roles is not an authority structure—although this is important—but rather a personal love relationship. As parents, therefore, we need to prioritize *positive love investment.*

Paul describes some of the key features of this positive love investment in one of his letters:

> 1 Thessalonians 2:[7] But we proved to be gentle among you, as a nursing *mother* tenderly cares for her own children. [8] Having so fond an affection for you, we were well-pleased to impart to you not only the gospel of God but also our own lives, because you had become very dear to us... [11] just as you know how we were exhorting and encouraging and imploring each one of you as a *father* would his own children...

Paul likens himself and his team as spiritual parents of the new Thessalonian Christians. He emphasizes that parenting involves both tender-hearted affection and positive encouragement. Passages like this suggest certain long-term relational goals we should have with our children:

- That they are basically confident that they are dear to us and that we are truly for them. Although this confidence must ultimately be rooted in God's love, parents play a major role in communicating this message to their children. They need this from us most in the early years, but we never "graduate" from this aspect of parenting!

- That they value their relationships with us enough that alienation from us is unnatural and undesirable. Overall and in the long run, we should bank on the influential power of our love relationship much more than our ability to control them. This is the tether that will be most likely to hold through the "white water" teen years. This is what will guide our corrective discipline so that it is most effective. This is the best motivator of our children's spiritual development.

- That they know how to form deep and lasting relationships with other people, and they see this as a key source of personal fulfillment—more than making money, school and sports and career achievement, and human prestige.

How can we work toward these goals? Here are some practical suggestions:

- Spend sufficient *quantity time* with your children. Research indicates that regular nurturing interaction with a relaxed affect is especially crucial with infants. Children who do not form secure attachments with their parents in infancy evidence a much higher rate of relational and emotional problems later in life.[2] This is

2 "In comparison with securely attached infants, those insecurely or anxiously attached are less competent and less sympathetic in interaction with their peers and less effective in eliciting and accepting help in problem-solving situations." Susan B. Crockenberg, "Infant Irritability, Mother Responsiveness, and Social Support Influences on the Security of Infant-

one reason why it is so desirable to have one parent at home most of the time with children before school age. If this is not possible, child-care that prioritizes genuine nurture is extremely important. Sufficient quantity time is a special challenge for American fathers, who generally allow work and hobbies to sap their time and emotional energy from their children. One study revealed that the average American father spends only 17 minutes a day in the physical proximity of his preschool children. The amount of time playing and personally interacting with children is far less. Another study (35 years old) revealed that the average father has only 2.7 such encounters per day, totaling only 37 seconds![3] I doubt that things have gotten much better!

- Invest *quality time* with your children. "Quality time" refers to meaningful interaction with your children over against mere physical proximity. Dr. Ross Campbell gives three very practical ways to do this: eye-contact, meaningful touch and focused attention.[4] We should also tell them frequently that we love them, praise their accomplishments, encourage them when they are faltering, and help them with their relational difficulties with others.

- Set up enjoyable *regular time* with your children. Adjust these times as your kids get older so they keep looking forward to them. I took my daughters out on weekly "dad and daughter dates" from the time they were able to walk until they had their own children.

Mother Attachment," in M. E. Heatherington and Ross, D. Parke, *Contemporary Readings in Child Psychology*, Third Edition (McGraw-Hill Book Company, 1988), p. 167.

[3] James Dobson, *Straight Talk to Men and Their Wives* (W Pub Group, 1980), p. 36

[4] Ross Campbell, *How To Really Love Your Child*

> We still go out every other week. When they were
> young, we went to their favorite fast-food places and
> ordered "happy meals." When they got older, we
> graduated to ordering their favorite appetizers from
> other restaurants. Today, we go to adult restaurants. I
> have no idea how much money I have spent doing
> this—but it has been worth every penny! Family
> vacations and other family traditions (like Thanksgiving
> and Christmas) also build a sense of belonging and
> family identity.

Are you willing to make career and financial and hobby sacrifices in
order to provide abundant positive love investment in your
children? Proverbs 15:17 says: "A bowl of vegetables with someone
you love is better than steak with someone you hate." How many of
us have paid the price of our parents' neglect in this crucial aspect
of parenting?

God can break this generational cycle and redeem our lives if we
cooperate with Him in investing love in our children! Yes, this is a
complicated area. No, there are not concrete rules about how much
you can work, what you buy, how often you move, how much debt
you can carry, etc. But you will need to lean strongly against our
culture's materialistic values in this area and make sacrifices to build
a relationship-centered life and pass this on to your children!

Corrective Discipline

The Bible teaches that children are both created in God's image and
born with a sinful nature that inclines them toward rebellion and
selfishness and deceit. This is why it emphasizes the importance of
corrective discipline, which is what Paul refers to in Ephesians 6:4
when he says "Bring them up in the... instruction of the Lord."
"Instruction" (*nouthesia*) is better translated "correction."

Many secular parenting "experts" reject childhood sinfulness and
therefore argue against the need for authoritative parental direction
and correction.

> "Empathy comes more easily when you see your role as a
> nurturer, with a large degree of faith in your child's capacity
> for self-direction. Empathy is more difficult when you
> believe you should direct and guide children, when you feel
> you... know best."[5]

> "'Nice,' 'good,' 'bad'... such labels have no place in the
> vocabulary of nurturing adults."[6]

Compare this to the biblical emphasis that corrective discipline is
needed and, when administered properly, is an important expression
of love.

> Proverbs 22:15 Foolishness is bound up in the heart of a
> child; the rod of discipline will remove it far from him.

> Proverbs 13:24 He who withholds his rod hates his son, but
> he who loves him disciplines him diligently.

Christians differ over whether Proverbs' "rod of discipline" requires
corporal punishment, or whether Solomon is speaking figuratively
of the principle of discipline, which takes many forms. But it is clear
that corrective discipline is a legitimate and important part of
parents' responsibility as delegated authorities over their children. It
can be abused, so we should implement measures to prevent
disciplinary abuse and be accountable to others for how we
discipline our children. But to reject corrective discipline because it
can be abused is a foolish reaction that deprives our children of
something they need from us.

5

[6] Dorothy Corkille Briggs. *Your Child's Self-esteem*, p. 86.

Here are some suggested long-term goals for our children in this area:

- That they realize that they are sinners who need both God's forgiveness through Christ and God's changing power through the Holy Spirit. In other words, we don't want our children to merely become externally compliant to biblical morality; we want them to see their need to depend on God to change their hearts. Therefore, corrective discipline combines pointing out the need to change with pointing to the Source of change—Jesus Christ.

- That they develop increasing self-control so they can enjoy their freedom to love people and serve God. As the chart below illustrates, we have to begin with almost entirely external control in early childhood. But the goal is for our children to develop an internal locus of control, so we should gradually expand it as they demonstrate self-control. The ideal is for them to have substantial freedom from our supervision by the time they leave our homes.

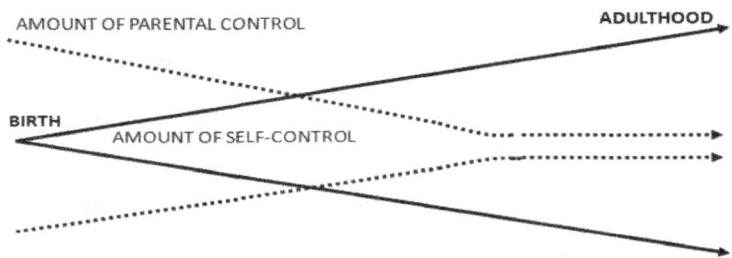

Some Christian parenting models advocate an excessively rigid, behavior-based form of training that under-emphasizes inner attitudes and the development of self-control. This often results in

children who are exasperated or provoked into rebellion.[7] Other
children of this parenting style are unable to cope with the sudden
freedom they have when they leave home, while still others remain
compliant and become self-righteous "older brothers."

- That they respect legitimate authority figures and can obey
  them with a good attitude most of the time. Without this,
  they will have big problems at school and at work, and their
  witness for Christ will suffer. On the other hand, we need
  not be too worried about disrespect toward us during the
  teenage years as long as it is within tolerable bounds. After
  all, we want a love relationship with them more than mere
  external compliance.

Sound corrective discipline is complicated and requires wisdom, but
it includes the following principles:

- It is *child-centered* rather than parent-centered. This
  means that our discipline should be motivated by what
  our child needs rather than by what we want or need.
  Examples of parent-centered parenting include:

  - Flying into a rage when our children
    accidentally break something we like

  - Neglecting discipline because it is inconvenient
    to us

  - Using guilt motivation to punish or manipulate

  - Lecturing to vent our frustration instead of
    devising an effective discipline

Since being parent-centered comes naturally to us as self-centered
people, we will need to continually lean against this tendency by

---

[7] See Paul's warning in Colossians 3:21 – "Fathers, do not exasperate your children, so that
they will not lose heart."

asking God: "What does my child need to learn? How can I best help him/her learn this?" We should also apologize to our children when we have been parent-centered in our discipline, and explain that we are committed with God's help to change in this area for their good.

- It is *age-appropriate* and *with explanation.* Wise parents utilize a broad range of corrective disciplines, including verbal correction, physical restriction, withdrawal of privileges, and non-intervention of natural consequences. We will need to adapt corrective discipline as our children develop in order to maximize its effectiveness.

  In general, young children require more direct intervention and physical restriction. Deliberate defiance of parents and anti-social treatment of peers call for this kind of prompt discipline after a warning. With older children, withdrawing privileges is often an effective way of correcting defiance or deceit, while allowing natural consequences to take their course can motivate them to become more faithful to their responsibilities.

  Overall, the aim of our discipline is to help our children realize the significance of their choices. By the time they leave our supervision, we hope to convince them that because their choices have consequences, they see the importance of making good choices.

  As early as possible, we need to explain the reasons why our discipline is for their good, and affirm that we discipline them because we love them. Even though they may reject this at the time, it is still important that they hear us explain and affirm. This will make it more difficult for them to believe that our discipline was capricious or malicious.

If they know that we have prayed and wrestled to do the right thing, they will likely remember this more than the specific discipline. God works through this effort on our parts to influence our children toward Him, the One we have been trying to follow as their parents.

- *It is consistent with biblical ethical priorities.* Some sinful attitudes and behaviors are far more harmful than others. We should make a bigger disciplinary deal of the more harmful matters, while being more lenient or even forbearing with lesser sins. We find these ethical priorities in the Bible. When the Bible repeats certain ethical themes, God is revealing that this is an ethical priority. Sometimes the Bible directly states that certain ethical issues are more important than others. Notice how Jesus rebukes the scribes and Pharisees for reversing God's ethical priorities:

Matthew 23:23 "Woe to you, scribes and Pharisees, hypocrites! For you tithe mint and dill and cummin, and have neglected *the weightier provisions of the law:* justice and mercy and faithfulness; but these are the things you should have done without neglecting the others."

It was OK for the scribes and Pharisees to give 10% of their garden herbs as part of their tax payment. But loving their neighbors by pursuing just treatment for them, forgiving them, and being consistently committed to their welfare was far more important.

In another passage, Jesus' enemies criticized Him for dining with tax collectors and other social undesirables. They emphasized ritual purity, and viewed contact with such people as ritual defilement. In response, Jesus quoted God's statement through the Old Testament prophet Hosea: "I desire compassion, and not a sacrifice." In other words, God prioritizes compassion toward lost people over ceremonial correctness.

Ethical priorities are important in corrective discipline, because our children sin in many ways every day—yet we can't discipline them for every sin without exasperating them (Colossians 3:21) or neglecting our other parenting priorities. So we have to try to discipline according to what is most ethically important. In general, this means that we should be heavier with sins like defiance, deceit, sexual impurity, substance abuse, and greed. How tragic when Christian parents make a big deal about their children using off-color language, but look the other way when they shun friends to gain social popularity! How tragic when they ground their children for under-performing academically, but show little or no concern when they neglect Christian fellowship! These responses reflect worldly values rather than biblical ethical priorities.

- *It is in addition to positive love investment rather than replacing it.* We need to keep initiating the positive love investment especially during the difficult times, even when they're making us pay a high price for disciplining them. To withdraw love investment as a discipline is hypocritical because this is not how God deals with us. It is also self-centered and very damaging. Here is an opportunity for us to "bless those who curse."

When one of my daughters was making destructive choices, we had to take a very strong disciplinary stand with her over a prolonged period of time. But I kept my weekly "Dad and daughter date" with her throughout this time. I tried to keep these times as positive as possible, although they were often personally painful for me. I wondered at the time if this made any difference because she continued on a wrong path. But later, she told me how those weekly dates helped to ultimately convince her to change her direction. She couldn't deny that she was loved in spite of our disapproval of her actions—and this fact became more influential over time.

As you think about your own parenting with reference to positive love investment and corrective discipline, you will probably notice certain weaknesses or sinful tendencies. In the chart below, the upper-right hand quadrant ("authoritative") is the ideal toward which we want to move; one of the other three quadrants is the place from which we are moving. Your spouse may have the same weakness, or she may have a very different weakness. If you can agree on the ideal, and agree on what each other's weaknesses are, you can prayerfully help one another and work together toward becoming more "authoritative" parents.

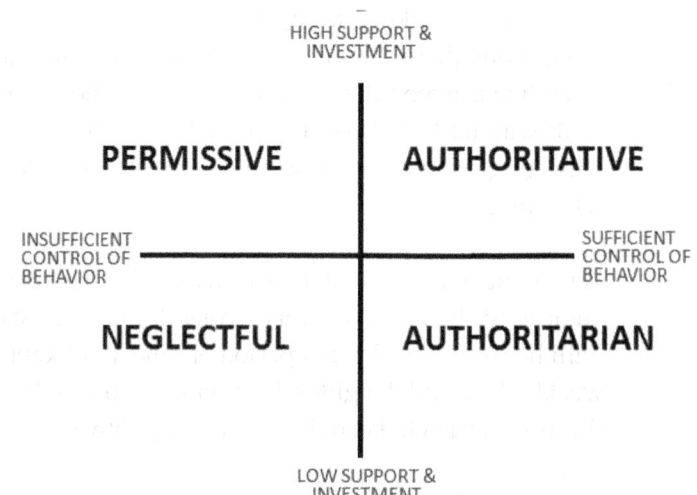

Spiritual Development

Our children are spiritual beings, created to enjoy a personal
relationship with God and to discover and fulfill His purpose for
their lives. And as parents, we are stewards—our children belong to
Him, and they are entrusted to us for a time to help them become His
life-long servants. We play a critical role of influence in our
children's spiritual development, for good or ill. Paul emphasizes
this responsibility in Ephesians 6:4b when he says "...bring them up
in the training and instruction of the Lord."

What should our long-term goals be in this crucial area? If we do
not have biblical goals for this aspect of our parenting and prioritize
them, we make our children extremely vulnerable to Satan's world-
system, which seduces people away from God and His values
(1 John 2:15-17). Tragically, many Christian parents have clear
sports and educational and career goals for their children, but draw
a blank on spiritual goals. It is not that the above goals are evil, but
unless they are superseded by and integrated into proper spiritual
goals, our children will usually become worldly by default. Consider
the following spiritual development goals:

- That they make an informed and genuine decision to
  receive Christ. We want our children to know the
  difference between learning about Jesus and personally
  receiving Him and asking Him to forgive their sins. We
  want them to choose their own relationship with Christ,
  and to be able to testify to the reality of this
  relationship.

- That they develop personal enjoyment of prayer, God's
  Word and Christian fellowship. Apart from a personal
  relationship with Christ, these things are merely
  external activities. But once they know Christ, these
  activities become the means through which we

experience Christ's love and power. We should insist
that our young children participate in these activities
even when they are aversive to them, but we should be
praying for the "dots to connect" so that they experience
the goodness of relating to God in these ways. We
should also do our best to make these activities fun and
enjoyable (see below).

- They are excited about a lifestyle of ministry—sharing
their faith, helping their Christian friends to grow
spiritually, and using their spiritual gifts to serve others.
The Christian life is about "faith working through love"
(Galatians 5:7). True fulfillment is the result of serving
others for Christ's sake (John 13:17). God protects our
children from the seductive power of sensuality and
materialism primarily by giving them real purpose and
satisfaction through this way of life.

How can we help our children toward these goals? Here are some
key steps we can take:[8]

- Model personal enthusiasm about relating to God and
serving Him. We adopt values not so much by what key
people teach us, as by when they relate enthusiastically to
what they teach us. When we teach that something is
important, but relate to it with boredom or complaint, our
children will likely become aversive to that value. If our
children perceive that we find God boring compared to
football games, or that we gather with other Christians only
out of duty, or that we complain about having to serve
others, we shouldn't be surprised when they decide this is
not the lifestyle they want.

---

[8] Some of these points are documented in the research of Dennis H. Dirks, "Moral Maturity
and Parenting," *Christian Education Journal,* Vol. 9, No. 2 (Winter, 1989), pp. 85–87.

For decades, our church has followed our children's involvement in fellowship from school years into adulthood. Not surprisingly, we find a very low dropout rate among children whose parents are committed to ministry within their home groups. We find a higher dropout rate among children whose parents are not involved in our church at all. But the highest dropout rate is among children whose parents are only nominally involved in our church. Nominal involvement sends a stronger negative message about church involvement than no involvement!

Don't interpret this point to mean that you must fake how you feel when your spiritual life is tough. You need to be able to process this honestly with Christian friends. But our children need to see us choosing to relate to things of God with a positive attitude even when we are struggling. They need to hear us express thankfulness for our lives with God even when we have sadness. They will learn through this that God is truly our greatest treasure, and this will attract them toward Him.

- Initiate frequent and informal spiritual interactions. What do our children learn about God if we only talk about Him at certain times, or if we use a different tone of voice or vocabulary when we talk to Him? They learn that a relationship with God is peripheral and formal—and this will likely turn them off to God. But when we talk to and about God with the same natural way we talk about other things that are important to us, our children learn that life with God is vital and personal.

Younger children usually want to learn from their parents. We should capitalize on this precious opportunity by initiating frequent interactions about God. Deuteronomy 6:7 describes this kind of interaction:

"You shall teach them (God's truths) diligently to your sons and shall talk of them when you sit in your house and when you walk by the way and when you lie down and when you rise up."

We can also create enjoyable regular times for spiritual interaction. When our daughters were little, I told them a Bible story and a "Daddy" story (of when I was their age) before praying with them at bed-time. They could never get enough of this—partly because it enabled them to stay up longer, but also because it somehow made life with God more real to them.

Things get more complicated as children enter into adolescence. They tend to be less receptive to their parents initiating conversations about God. We have to wait more for when they initiate—and then be careful not to sound too excited! We have to expect to be tested by objections, and we dare not react with visible distress when they express doubts. We want to help them make their faith their own, not insist that they conform so that we feel safe or look good to others.

Since peers and other adults play much bigger influencing roles at this stage, we should encourage and facilitate connections with adults and peers who are spiritually-minded. This is one reason why a vital student ministry is so critical for our children's spiritual development. Don't crowd their schedules excessively with sports, academics, and other activities. Give them lots of time be influenced by God through the adults and peers He has placed in their lives.

- Pray for them consistently and according to biblical
  priorities. Intercessory prayer according to God's will
  unleashes God's redemptive power into people's lives. All
  effective spiritual work is birthed and bathed in prayer. Yet
  it is easy to be so busy with other aspects of parenting that
  we neglect this strongest spiritual influence on our
  children. Consider the following biblical parental prayer
  priorities:

Hanna gave her son Samuel to the Lord while he was still a baby
(1 Samuel 1:11), and Job prayed regularly for his children's spiritual
welfare (Job 1:5). We should pray in similar ways for our children.

Paul prayed for God to open the Ephesian Christians' hearts to
understand their hope-filled future, their preciousness to God and
the greatness of God's power available to them (Ephesians 1:18,19).
How our children need this kind of revelation! Only God can give it
to them, and He gives it in answer to our prayers.

James urges us to pray for God's wisdom (James 1:5). We want to
accurately communicate God's truth and love to our children
concerning every major issue of life. We can't deliver godliness as a
formula; we have to go to God situation by situation and get the
wisdom we need.

When our children are straying from God, we need to pray for God's
interventional exposure and discipline to show them the emptiness
of a life of sin. God's promise to discipline wayward Israel can be the
basis for our prayers for our wayward children:

Hosea 2:6 "Therefore, behold, I will hedge up her way with thorns, and I
will build a wall against her so that she cannot find her paths. [7] She
will pursue her lovers, but she will not overtake them; and she will
seek them, but will not find them. Then she will say, 'I will go back
to my first husband, for it was better for me then than now!'"

Someone told me many years ago: "Parenting is not for the faint of heart!" Thirty-two years of being a parent has proven to me the profound truth of this statement. How we need God's provision to play this precious role! We need His abundant forgiveness for our many parental sins and errors. We need the new identity He gives us in Christ so that we don't try to get our identity from our children's performance. We need our brothers and sisters in Christ for advice and support every step of the way. We need God's power to redeem the disappointments and spiritual attacks that our children will sustain. May God teach us to come to Him on the basis of His grace to receive these promised provisions – so we can parent our children toward Him.

Chapter 16
Colossians 3:22-4:1 The Path to Spiritual Maturity — Part #8

Christians at Work

Much of Paul's letter to the Colossians is theological, but this is the practical part, in which he explains what Christianity should look like at home and at work. He began this section by enunciating a key principle:

> [3, 17] Whatever you do in word or deed, do all in the name of the Lord Jesus, giving thanks through Him to God the Father.

Jesus does not want His followers to separate their lives into spiritually important and unimportant parts. Rather, He wants us to represent Him and serve Him in every area of our lives. We need this reminder because we tend to live one way within the church and another way at home and at work. O. Hallesby makes this observation about Christians in Norway in the 1930's:

> "We find (Christians) in responsible positions (at work) who in their daily lives are peevish and imperious and in whom their subordinates observe very little conscientiousness, not to speak of Christianity. Even less do they see any zeal for the salvation of the immortal souls in their employ. But outside, in Christian organizations of various kinds, these men are zealous for... evangelism, and many such things. We find employees who studiously avoid more work than they are strictly compelled to do. Clock-watchers and time-stealers. Difficult to get along with. They will not stand (to be)

corrected, and become pouty and peevish upon the least
provocation. Their superiors see little conscientiousness on
their part, and even less zeal for the immortal souls with
whom they are associated from day to day... But they are
zealous in such special Christian enterprises as... evangelistic
meetings, prayer meetings, etc. They live their lives on two
planes, a religious and a secular... Our great temptation –
and it is common to us all – is to neglect everyday
Christianity."[1]

Do you identify with this struggle? I know I do! In this chapter, we
will study what Paul and other New Testament authors say about
Christians at work.

[3, 22] Slaves, in all things obey those who are your masters on
earth, not with external service, as those who merely please
men, but with sincerity of heart, fearing the Lord. [23]
Whatever you do, do your work heartily, as for the Lord
rather than for men, [24] knowing that from the Lord you will
receive the reward of the inheritance. It is the Lord Christ
whom you serve. [25] For he who does wrong will receive the
consequences of the wrong which he has done, and that
without partiality. [4,1] Masters, grant to your slaves justice
and fairness, knowing that you too have a Master in heaven.

Paul's instructions to slaves and masters do not imply that human
slavery is ethical. He applies biblical principles to this social
structure without commenting on its morality. It is true that the
Bible has been tragically used to justify slavery; it also true that the
Bible's high view of all humans as God's image-bearers eventually
led to the abolition of slavery in the western world.

---

[1] O. Hallesby, *Under His Wings,* (Saint Andrew Press, 1978), p. 84,86.

There are important differences between slavery in the Greco-Roman world and slavery in 18th and 19th century United States. Likewise, there are important differences between slave-master relationships and employee-employer relationships. But the principles that Paul emphasizes in this passage apply to both situations.

Unbiblical views of work

Before looking closely at what this passage *does* say about work, we should notice what it does *not* say. Paul views work in a radically different way than most American Christians view it. Consider:

- There is nothing here about getting our identity from our job position ("I am a doctor, carpenter, lawyer, plumber, etc."). This is because Christians already have a new identity as God's children that has nothing to do with their job roles.

  Colossians 3:[10] (You) have put on the new self who is being renewed to a true knowledge according to the image of the One who created him— [11] a renewal in which there is no distinction between Greek and Jew, circumcised and uncircumcised, barbarian, Scythian, slave and freeman, but Christ is all, and in all.

  So we don't work *for* an identity; we work *from* our identity in Christ. Any time we look to our jobs to give us a foundational sense of identity or significance, we have moved away from biblical teaching.

- There is nothing here about finding the job that suits our talents and interests. This isn't wrong, but it was simply not an option for many of these Christians because they were slaves who had little or no job mobility. Although we are not slaves, many of us have limited job options. But as we will see, Paul teaches that all Christians can still live significant and rewarding lives regardless of what kinds of jobs we have.

Rather, Paul focuses on four key issues: For *Whom* we work, *what* should characterize our work, *why* we should this work way, and *how* God empowers us to work this way.

For Whom we work

The first order of business is being clear about the Person for Whom we work. Although Paul acknowledges that these Christians either serve "masters according to the flesh" (3:22) or are "masters" (4:1), he emphasizes that they all work for the same unseen ("heavenly") Master. This is not just some fluffy religious slogan. Jesus has been raised from the dead. He is now Lord over every one of His followers, and He is Lord over every area of our lives, including our jobs. So you may have a human supervisor at work, but Jesus is the One you ultimately serve (3:22,23,24). You may supervise others at work, but Jesus is the One to whom you are ultimately accountable (4:1). This fact should radically change our attitude toward our jobs in three ways:

- Whatever job we have, it is an arena in which we worship Jesus. In 3:17, Paul says that whatever we do (including our work), we should do giving thanks to the Father through Jesus. Thanksgiving is central to New Testament worship, as the author of Hebrews says:

  Hebrews 13:[15] Through Him then, let us *continually* offer up a sacrifice of praise to God, that is, the fruit of lips that give thanks to His name.

  This thankful attitude in the midst of our difficult jobs is worship just as meaningful as when we give thanks at a meeting with other Christians. This perspective is consistent with the New Testament's teaching that that our entire lifestyle should be an ongoing worship service.

Romans 12.[1] Therefore I urge you, brethren, by the mercies of God, to present your bodies a living and holy sacrifice, acceptable to God, which is your spiritual service of worship.

Our attitude and conduct at work is therefore no less a part of our worship of Jesus than our private prayer times.

- Whatever our job is, it is an arena in which we represent Jesus to the watching world. To do something "in the name of" Jesus is to do it on His behalf, as His representative. This is why the New Living Translation translates Colossians 3.17, "Whatever you do or say, do it as a representative of the Lord Jesus." We spend many hours every week at work. If the work-place is not an arena in which we are intentionally influencing people toward Jesus, we are putting our lights under a basket (Matthew 5.14-16)! Our attitude and conduct at work is therefore no less a part of our witness for Jesus than our participation in a short-term missions trip or outreach ministry.

- Whatever our jobs are, we ultimately serve a gracious Master. Paul spent the first two chapters of this letter expounding how gracious Jesus is and how secure we are in His love. This foundation can liberate us from some of the most burdensome aspects of the work-place. We do not need to live in crippling anxiety over work-related criticism or performance evaluations. They are not a threat to our identity or security, because we know who we are in Christ and we know He will meet our deepest needs. We do not need to resort to flattery and favor-currying to get approval or validation from our supervisors or work associates. We

already have Jesus' approval and we work from His
approval to please Him. We don't have to view our current
jobs as something we're stuck in, or as the present step up
the career ladder. Rather, they are temporary assignments
in our lives with the Lord—assignments that He may
change in the future according to His good plans for us.

Do you belong to Jesus? If you don't, you are missing out on a
relationship with the only Person who can integrate every aspect of
your life. Without Jesus, your life will be fragmented into
unconnected and even contradictory compartments. But if you ask
the living Jesus to be your Savior and Lord, He will begin to show
you how every area of your life—including your work—can have
meaning and significance through Him.

If you do belong to Jesus, ask Him to burn it into your consciousness
and remind you daily that you serve Him at work.

What should characterize our work

Since if we belong to Jesus we work for Him, what should
characterize our work? Paul gives us three answers to that question
in this passage, and I'll add two more answers from other New
Testament passages.

- *We should respect and cooperate with our human
  supervisors* (3:22). This respect and submission is more
  than reluctant compliance to their directives. It involves
  proactively getting behind their legitimate work goals and
  creatively seeking to accomplish them. We should exhibit
  this attitude not only to their faces, but also in the break
  room when they are not around. We should choose this
  attitude even if they are unreasonable, as Peter says
  expressly:

1 Peter 2:[18] Servants, be submissive to your masters with all respect, not only to those who are good and gentle, but also to those who are unreasonable.

Of course, we can disagree with our supervisors over work-related issues, and at times even offer our input. We must also be willing to disobey our supervisors if they command us to do things that the Lord forbids. But disrespecting, sabotaging, arguing with, or passively resisting our supervisors is rebelling against Jesus, because He asks us to do this as part of our work for Him.

- *We should work hard* (3:23), whether we are recognized and/or rewarded for our hard work or not. We aren't doing our work merely for a raise or promotion; we are doing it for the Lord. Showing up late, taking off early, or loafing on the job are insubordination to the One who worked hard for our salvation when we deserved only His condemnation.

- *We should treat those we employ or oversee with justice and fairness* (4:1). We should not abuse our authority by disrespecting or taking advantage of those we oversee. Rather, we should exemplify a servant-leader attitude, because Jesus is our Master and He used His authority to serve rather than to exploit us.

- *We should have a willing, helpful demeanor,* as Paul says elsewhere:

  Ephesians 6:7 With good will render service, as to the Lord, and not to men...

  Philippians 2:14 Do all things without grumbling or disputing...

  The workplace is often dominated by grumbling, complaining, gossiping, and other forms of negativity. By contrast, we should be major contributors to good work-place morale!

- *We should be trustworthy,* as Paul says elsewhere:

  Titus 2:9 9 Urge bond-slaves to be... [10] not pilfering, but showing all good faith...

  This means, of course, that we should come to work consistently and on time. We should not steal from the work-place, either by taking materials or by killing time. Our supervisors and work-associates should be able to trust us to be honest about work-related matters.

Because you work for Jesus, you should be an exemplary worker in the above ways. Your supervisors and associates should be glad that you work for and with them. If you work this way, you will more likely be promoted because such employees are very difficult to find today! And yet (also because you work for Jesus) you should be known as one who does not live for your job, who can and does set work boundaries so that your job does not undermine your family and church responsibilities, and who is willing to leave your job if Jesus calls you into other roles of service for Him.

Why we should work this way

Working this way day in and day out is not easy; it requires adequate motivation! In addition to the primary motivation that we work for Jesus, the New Testament gives us four additional motivations for doing our work this way:

- *Through work God provides us with the financial means to support ourselves and our families, and to give to the church and to people who are in need.*

  2 Thessalonians 3:7 For you yourselves know how you ought to follow our example, because... [8] (we) did not eat anyone's

bread without paying for it, but with labor and hardship we kept working night and day so that we would not be a burden to any of you; [9] ... order to offer ourselves as a model for you, so that you would follow our example. [10] For even when we were with you, we used to give you this order: if anyone is not willing to work, then he is not to eat, either.

1 Timothy 5:8 But if anyone does not provide for his own, and especially for those of his household, he has denied the faith...

1 Corinthians 16:1 Now concerning the collection for the saints, as I directed the churches of Galatia, so do you also. [2] On the first day of every week each one of you is to put aside and save, as he may prosper...

Ephesians 4:28 He who steals must steal no longer; but rather he must labor, performing with his own hands what is good, so that he will have something to share with one who has need.

As we saw earlier, the New Testament says nothing about seeking a career that suits your talents or vocational interests. It does not forbid doing this as long as this does not lead you to compromise God's other priorities for your life. But this was simply not an option for most first-century Christians, either because they were slaves or because they had little work liberty. Likewise, this has not been an option for most Christians over the past two thousand years.

Rather, the New Testament urges us to base our significance on our new identity in Christ, and on the ministries which God has given us to build up His church. This will result in a deep sense of significance, while looking for significance in our careers is a project that is sure to ultimately disappoint us.[2]

But work does provide us with a means of material sustenance for our own selves and for our families. And if we live simply, work also provides us with means to give financially to support the work of the church and to help needy people. In other words, work provides us with a means to practically love the people God has put into our lives. This is a wonderful provision for which we should be truly thankful, and which should motivate us to work hard! But there is more.

- *At work we can attract people to Jesus or repel them from Jesus.* By being good employees we can make the gospel attractive.

  Titus 2:9 Urge bond-slaves to be subject to their own masters in everything, to be well-pleasing, not argumentative, [10] not pilfering, but showing all good faith *so that they will adorn the doctrine of God our Savior in every respect.*

By being good employees, we can also expose by positive contrast the darkness and emptiness of life without Jesus, and we can offer the refreshing news about Jesus.

  Philippians 2:14 Do all things without grumbling or disputing; [15] *so that you will prove yourselves to be blameless and innocent, children of God above reproach in the midst of a crooked and perverse generation, among whom you appear as lights in the world,* [16] *holding forth the word of life...*

---

[2] Paul warns Christians 1 Timothy 6:9,10 not to seek material wealth because this will result in serious personal injury. The disappointment of seeking one's significance though career is one example of this injury.

On the other hand, we can discredit Christianity by being poor workers.

> 1 Timothy 6:1 All who are under the yoke as slaves are to regard their own masters as worthy of all honor *so that the name of God and our doctrine will not be spoken against.*

Each year I am deeply saddened to hear of cases in which people are turned off to Christianity because of Christians who commonly lie or gossip or loaf or bully at work. Thank God that I also hear of people who are attracted to Jesus because of Christians who represent Him well at work!

The great majority of Americans are now unchurched. They have never attended Christian churches or Bible studies. They do not have Christian friends or family members. They will not respond to billboards or websites that invite them to Christian churches. The media often misrepresents Christianity, and Christian hypocrites confirm their suspicions. All of this means that one of the few ways Americans will ever come into contact with the living Jesus is through Christians at work. We will study in a later chapter how to share our faith in Jesus, but our supervisors and work-associates must see a positive difference in our lives at work if we expect them to take the message about Jesus seriously!

- *God wants to shape our character through our work-place.*

> Romans 8:28 We know that God causes all things to work together for good to those who love God, to those who are called according to His purpose.

One of the "all things" God works through to conform us to Christ's image is the work-place! And it is especially the difficult people and distasteful circumstances at work that God wants to use toward this end!

God challenged me with this truth as a young Christian, and it
changed the way I viewed my job. At the time, I worked as a busboy
and dishwasher and cook. I began to ask the Lord: "What character
lessons are You trying to teach me here?" As I began to focus on this
question and respond to His answers, He helped me to focus less on
the difficult people with whom I worked and the many other
distasteful aspects of my job. I also began to see how what I was
learning at work was helping me to become a better Christian
worker. He used later jobs to help me become a better son to my
parents and a better room-mate. The ten years I worked at jobs like
this were also crucial preparation for marriage, parenting, and
vocational Christian ministry. What character lesson is God trying to
teach you through your current job?

- *Jesus will reward us well for serving Him at work.*

  Colossians 3:24... knowing that from the Lord you will
  receive the reward of the inheritance. It is the Lord Christ
  whom you serve.

  Ephesians 6:7 With good will render service, as to the Lord,
  and not to men, [8] knowing that whatever good thing each
  one does, this he will receive back from the Lord, whether
  slave or free.

These verses evidently refer to Jesus' evaluation of our service for
Him when He returns. This is our ultimate *performance evaluation*.
Every way we let Him transform us through work, everything we do
did to represent Him well to others at work will be recalled and
honored and rewarded in ways that will ripple through all eternity.
This is our ultimate *compensation package* – and it will be based on
our faithfulness, not our job status. There will be Christian
dishwashers who are richly rewarded, and Christian executives who
are not rewarded at all! How often do you think about your job as an
opportunity for eternal reward?

How God empowers us to work this way

We not only need motivation to do our work this way. We also need supernatural empowerment. Paul doesn't directly address this issue in our passage, but the immediate context informs us of two key ways we can appropriate Jesus' power to serve Him at work.

- *Be vitally involved in Christian community.* As we saw in an earlier chapter, the previous paragraph (3:12-16) is an exhortation to live in loving unity with other Christians. In the New Testament letters, this exhortation to live in Christian community almost always comes immediately before exhortation to live our social roles in a way that accurately represents Christ.[3] Why? *Because we must be deeply involved with other Christians life in order to play these roles effectively.* You cannot be a good employee, manager, spouse or parent. unless you are truly engaged with your Christian brothers and or sisters!

This is where you get spiritually built up to go into the often spiritually-draining workplace. This is where you get prayer to be a witness at work. This is where you get advice about how to handle work challenges in a godly way. This is where you get insight on how God is trying to transform your character at work.

This is why you should do your best to work your job around your involvement in Christian fellowship, rather than work your involvement in fellowship around your job. Are you willing to hold the line on how many hours you are willing to work so you can be vitally involved in fellowship? Are you willing to ask for schedule adjustments for this purpose? Are you willing to look for another job to safeguard adequate involvement in Christian community? If you are an excellent worker, employers are often willing to adjust your

---

[3] See also Romans 12,13, Ephesians 5,6, and 1 Peter 1-3.

schedule in order to keep you. If you pray consistently for this, God will eventually provide ways for you to do it because this is His will for your life!

- *Talk to Jesus about work* (4:2). The following context links our work lives to prayer.

   Colossians 4:2 Devote yourselves to prayer, keeping alert in it with an attitude of thanksgiving;

You work for Jesus – and Jesus is always present at work, not only to inspect your work, but also to empower you to work in a way that represents Him well. As you go to work daily, present yourself to Him as His servant and ask Him for the energy and love and respect and good will that you need. As challenges and opportunities arise at work, turn to Him in prayer for what you need to represent Him well. And remember to thank Him that He is with at work with you every step of the way.

We should also pray with and for one another along these lines. In our home group's weekly prayer meeting, we pray regularly for opportunities to share Christ with non-Christians at our jobs. We also pray for the Lord's help to work with the attitudes described above, so that we can arouse people's curiosity about this positive difference. We also pray for better jobs to enable us to be more generous financial givers. We have seen amazing answers as we pray regularly along these lines!

What kind of impact might Jesus have in our city if most of us served and represented Him at work in this way! Imagine that Christians at your work-place had the reputation as the most helpful, hardest working, kindest, employees. Imagine that your employers and supervisors work-associates recognized this. They may think that Christianity is nonsense, but they would want to hire and work with Christians. And chances are that at a certain point they would begin to ask themselves, "I wonder why these Christians are so different." How many more of these people might be receptive to conversations about Jesus? How many more of them might eventually receive Jesus? How many more of them might join us in Christian fellowship and begin to grow in their faith? No wonder the New Testament makes such a big deal about this!

Chapter 17
Colossians 4:2-6
The Path to Spiritual Maturity — Part #9

Representing Jesus in What We Say

Introduction

Paul was a highly gifted evangelist who commonly preached to large crowds of strangers. Most of the Colossian Christians were not like Paul in this regard. Likewise, most of us are more like the Colossians than Paul—normal people working and living and recreating among a relatively small number of people who don't yet know Christ (see diagram).

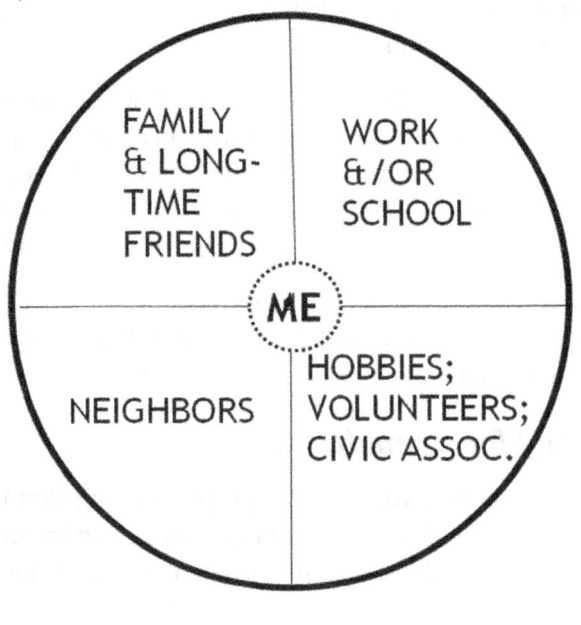

Nevertheless, Paul sees our evangelistic roles as both significant and full of potential. This is our unique sphere of influence. The key is for us to represent Jesus accurately among these people—both in what we do and what we say.

3, 17 Whatever you do in word or deed, do all in the name of the Lord Jesus, giving thanks through Him to God the Father.

"What we do" refers to our behavior and attitude as we relate to our neighbors, work associates, friends and family members. Paul describes this Colossians 3:18-4:1, and we have considered this in some detail in the previous three chapters. What a challenge to live this way! We should be asking God each day for His motivation and love and power to influence these people toward Jesus.

"What we say" refers to representing Jesus in the words we communicate. Elsewhere, Paul says that we are Jesus' ambassadors. Jesus has paid for everyone's sins, and He wants everyone to be reconciled to Him. So we want to tell the people in our spheres of influence about what He has done for them, and urge them to be reconciled to Him.

> 2 Corinthians 5: 20 Therefore, we are ambassadors for Christ, as though God were making an appeal through us: "We beg you on behalf of Christ, be reconciled to God. 21 He made Him who knew no sin to be sin on our behalf, so that we might become the righteousness of God in Him."

How can we represent Jesus well by "what we say?" In this passage Paul gives us three guidelines that will help us to be good ambassadors for Christ.

Pray for open doors

> Devote yourselves to prayer, keeping alert in it with an attitude of thanksgiving; 3 praying at the same time for us as well, that God will open up to us a door for the word, so that

we may speak forth the mystery of Christ, for which I have
also been imprisoned; [4] that I may make it clear in the way I
ought to speak. (Colossians 4: 2-4)

Telling people in our spheres of influence about Jesus usually begins
not by talking to them, but by talking to God. Specifically, it begins
with asking God for "open doors"—opportunities to speak about
Jesus.

Paul asks the Colossians to pray for open doors for him even though
he was imprisoned and cut off from normal social interaction. He
knew that God was willing and able to create these opportunities in
answer to prayer. Assuming that Paul wrote to the Philippian
Christians after this letter, we know at least part of the answer to the
Colossians' prayers.

> Now I want you to know, brethren, that my circumstances
> have turned out for the greater progress of the gospel, [13] so
> that my imprisonment in the cause of Christ has become
> well known throughout the whole praetorian guard and to
> everyone else... (Philippians 1:12-13)

"Praetorian" guards were Roman soldiers who guarded imperial
prisoners like Paul. Chained to them at all times, Paul found a
"captive audience" as they asked him why he was in custody! These
soldiers evidently told other Praetorian guards about Paul's faith.
And some of them probably received Christ because at the end of
Philippians, Paul sends greetings from Christians "of Caesar's
household" (Philippians 4:22).

If God can open doors for Paul even though he was imprisoned,
certainly He can open doors for us! This is why Paul not only asks
the Colossians to pray for open doors for him; he also implies in 4:2
that they should pray for open doors for themselves.

Seeing God answer prayers for open doors makes following Jesus an exciting adventure! Just this past week, God gave me two open doors (at least, two that I noticed). One was so surprising that I almost fumbled the ball. I was a little more ready for the other one, but it was just as exciting as the one that surprised me.

Do you pray regularly for open doors for *yourself?* James says that often we do not have simply because we do not ask God (James 4:2). Think what might happen if you got in the habit of asking God for this at the start of each day! The more you ask, the more doors God will open. The more doors God opens, the more motivated you will be to ask—and to look eagerly each day for the next answer.

Do you pray regularly for open doors for *one another?* Paul doesn't just pray for open doors for himself; he asks the Colossians to pray for this for him. The best way to do this is by praying regularly with your Christian friends, and making this kind of prayer a key priority. This is probably what Paul is calling them to do in 4:2.[1] We do this in our home group's weekly prayer meeting, and it is exciting to hear on a regular basis how God has answered this prayer. Think what might happen if you pray with other Christians every week along these lines!

When we pray for open doors, God will answer our prayers. What do we do when He answers? How do we talk about Jesus when He gives us this opportunity? Paul gives us two important guidelines...

Make the most of the opportunity

Conduct yourselves with wisdom toward outsiders, making the most of the opportunity. (Colossians 4:5)

---

[1] The immediately preceding and following context of Colossians 4:2 is about representing Jesus well among non-Christians. Therefore, Paul probably means: "Devote yourselves to prayer for effective outreach to people far from God. Keep alert in making these requests, and keep giving thanks as God answers them."

When God gives you an open door, make the most of the opportunity! "Make the most of" (*exagorazo*) is a market-place word (*agora* means "market-place"). It means to capitalize on a good deal. When I see a good deal on asparagus at the grocery store, I make the most of the opportunity by buying two bunches and making extra asparagus soup. When my wife saw a birthday gift for our grand-daughter was two-thirds off, she made the most of that opportunity by buying an extra one for our other grand-daughter's Christmas gift. When God gives you an opportunity to say something about Jesus, you should make the most of it!

In order to make the most of the opportunity, you need to "conduct yourself with wisdom." Biblical wisdom involves skill in doing God's will learned from observation and practice. A script will never do. We need wisdom because each opportunity is different—different people, different time available, different levels of interest, different degrees of credibility—so each opportunity requires a different verbal response.

- *It may be that people are so impressed by the way you live that they ask you why you are this way.* The is ideal scenario! Peter envisions non-Christians observing that Christians have hope within them, and asking them to explain why they have this hope.

  Sanctify Christ as Lord in your hearts, always being ready to make a defense to everyone who asks you to give an account for the hope that is in you, yet with gentleness and reverence... (1 Peter 3:15)

The people in our day-to-day spheres of influence should see something positively different about us that arouses their curiosity. It may be our hope in the midst of a difficult situation. It may be our hard-working servant attitude. It may be our refusal to join in with gossip or complaint. If people never ask you this kind of question, it

may be because you are ignoring Paul's instruction in Colossians
3:18-4:1! At any rate, when people compliment us for such things,
we shouldn't steal the credit for ourselves. We should give the credit
to Jesus, because He is the One who has changed us! This honest,
humble response often leads to additional opportunities to talk more
about our faith in Jesus.

- *It may be simply being honest about the subject you're
  talking about.* If I'm asked what books I like to read,
  honesty dictates that my answer include the spiritual
  books I'm reading. When my non-Christian friend asked
  me recently about how I was doing as my mother was
  dying, honesty dictated that I talk not only about my
  sadness, but also about my relief that because she knew
  Jesus we would see each other again. He responded to
  this by saying, "I wish I had that hope"—and I got to
  share how he could get it!

How do you respond when a non-Christian friend asks you to hang
out on an evening that you spend at a Bible study? Do you mumble,
"I can't; I'm busy"—or do you say, "I'd love to join you, but I go to a
Bible study that is so meaningful to me that I don't want to miss it." If
this is the truth, say it! This may arouse curiosity in your friend, or it
may not. But you made the most of an opportunity to say something
about your relationship with Christ.

- *It may be correcting a common misconception about
  Christianity.* The four most common misconceptions are:

  "Christianity is about performing religious
  observances"—instead of responding to Jesus' invitation
  to begin a love-relationship with Him (see Galatians
  4:4-11).

  "Christianity says I must earn God's acceptance by my
  good works"—instead of receiving His total forgiveness

as a free gift through simple faith in Jesus (see Ephesians 2:8,9).

"Christianity says I must change myself before I can come to Jesus"—instead of coming to Him as we are and letting Him transform us (see John 4:7-14).

"Christianity requires faith free from all doubts"—instead coming to Jesus with the little faith we have (see Mark 9:24).

You should assume that people have one or more of these misconceptions, and seek to discover which ones they have. If you defend your faith in Christ (see below) without first correcting these misconceptions, you are defending something you don't even believe! Instead, try asking people what they believe Christianity teaches about salvation, and then gently correct their misconceptions with the good news.

- *It may be doing your best to answer a question or objection about Christianity.* 1 Peter 3:15 (see above) urges us to "make a defense" in response to such questions or objections. If you know a proper answer, give it. If you don't, say, "That's a great question, but I don't know the answer. I'll investigate and let you know what I discover." We should welcome such questions, even when asked with a hostile or mocking attitude, because God may use our answers to impact the questioner or others who are listening.

- *It may be sharing how you became a Christian.* As we saw in Chapter 1, you are the world's foremost expert on your own story, and God speaks powerfully through our personal stories to attract people to Christ. The New Testament strongly emphasizes this way of talking about

Jesus.[2] In addition, people in our culture are generally
more receptive to such sharing than to argument or
debate about such matters. Look for ways to share
appropriately what misconceptions about Christianity
you had (see above), what you learned that corrected
these misconceptions, what biblical verses clarified the
good news for you, what personal needs led you to
consider turning to Christ, how you received Christ, and
how Christ has changed your life. God can use even one
sentence of your personal story to help others toward
His Son. I know, because He used brief comments like
this to reach me!

- *It may be giving someone a relevant book or recorded
  teaching for private use.* Some people who are
  unwilling to discuss Christianity with you in person
  may read or listen to a good Christian book or teaching
  in private. Over the years, I have met dozens of people
  who came to faith in Christ this way.

- *It may be inviting someone to attend a Bible study, or to
  socialize with your Christian friends.* Most people who
  respond to my invitation to a Bible study at our church
  are pleasantly surprised at how different it was from
  what they expected—even if I made it clear beforehand
  that it is not "churchy." This is not because the people in
  our church are so awesome—it is because hearing

---

[2] "Witness" (*marturo*) is the main word Jesus uses to describe our evangelistic mission
(Jn. 15,27; Acts 1,8)—and it means "give your testimony." The gospel of John emphasizes the
primary role of personal testimony (see for example Jn. 1,41,45; 9,1-34;20,31). Luke features
Paul's testimony 3 times in Acts (9,22,26), and uses *diamarturomai* ("solemnly testify" –
under-oath testimony) many times to describe Peter and Paul's preaching (Acts 2,40; 8,25;
10,42; 18,5; 20,21; 28,23). Rev. 12,11 emphasizes that we overcome the Serpent's deception
by "the word of our testimony." 1 Pet. 3,15, a text often cited to emphasize the importance of
apologetics, presumes that we have shared about the hope that we have so that people ask us
to give an account for this hope.

God's Word and seeing Christians loving one another
has a magnetic effect on open-hearted people. For this
reason, invitations to Bible studies are preferable. If
people decline this invitation, they may respond to an
invitation to a social event with your Christian
friends—and still get a chance to see Christian love and
hear about Jesus.

- *It may be challenging someone who has enough
  information to personally receive Christ.* My guess is
  that many of you had to be challenged in this way
  (maybe several times) before you entrusted yourself to
  Christ. Even though some Christians are premature
  about doing this, or insensitive in the way they do this,
  we should be willing to issue this challenge when
  needed. After all, most of us are more likely to be too
  timid than too bold!

How do you determine the best specific way to make the most of the
opportunity? Remember, Paul says we need wisdom. Wisdom here
probably refers not just to skill from observation and practice, but
also to wisdom imparted by the Holy Spirit to say what needs to be
said in the situation.[3] We can ask for His wisdom on the spot, and He
will give it to us! I call this "double-listening"—listening to the
person while at the same time asking God for wisdom to respond
properly. Ask God for this wisdom, and then share what you think
He wants you to say. Over time, you will become more confident that
God will supply you with the wisdom you need.

---

[3] Paul earlier prayed for the Colossians that they would be filled with spiritual wisdom so they
could represent Jesus well (1:9,10a). Paul has just asked them to pray that God would give him
the wisdom to "make it clear in the way I ought to speak" when God opens a door for him
(4:4). Jesus promised His disciples that the Holy Spirit would give them wisdom to answer
when challenged about their faith (Luke 21:15). Peter received Spirit-filled wisdom when
questioned by the Sanhedrin (Acts 4:8-12), as did Stephen when he was questioned by the
Synagogue of Freedmen (Acts 6:10).

Many Christians think that unless they get to explain the whole plan of salvation and issue a challenge to receive Christ, what they say "doesn't count." How wrong this is! Every single thing we say about Jesus with Spirit-led wisdom makes an impact! Each spiritual conversation I had with sincere Christians over a five-year period was like a link in a long chain that eventually led to my decision to receive Christ.

So pray for opportunities to talk about Jesus, and then make them most of them—and count on the fact that God will use what you said!

Speak graciously

> Let your speech always be with grace, as though seasoned with salt, so that you will know how you should respond to each person. (Colossians 4:6)

Paul tells us here that just as important as *what* we say about Jesus is *how* we say it. "With grace" probably describes how we should speak about Jesus. Gracious speech is a manner of conversing that is gentle and respectful ("Be ready to answer... yet with gentleness and respect" – 1 Peter 3:15). Paul says we should *always* speak graciously, no matter ungracious the other person may be.

What does this gracious speech look like? It is becoming a very rare commodity in our increasingly rude and self-absorbed culture. But for this very reason, we will stand out positively if we converse this way.

- *It means showing genuine warmth and courtesy in your normal, everyday interactions.* Francis Schaeffer said that even if we encounter someone only at a cross-walk, we should treat him well because he is made in God's image. Is it rare or common for you to be grouchy with work-associates, or rude with your family members, or aloof with your neighbors? Listen to what Paul says:

Do all things without grumbling or disputing; [15] so that you will prove yourselves to be... children of God above reproach in the midst of a crooked and perverse generation, among whom you appear as lights in the world....
(Philippians 2:14)

Ask God to help you to show His kindness to people in this simple but powerful way!

- *It means listening with genuine other-centered curiosity.* I call this "delighting in discovering another person." Few Christians are capable of having an entire conversation just finding out about the other person, and fewer still enjoy doing this! Instead, we are often self-absorbed, talking mainly about ourselves and easily bored with what others share. Other-centered listening is an expression of love, because it expresses the kind of interest that God has in people. As a young Christian, a mentor told me: "The most interest*ing* person is the most interest*ed* person." How true this is! Doors often swing open to speak about our faith when we listen carefully and patiently.

- *It means usually sharing rather than declaring.* There is certainly a place in one-on-one conversations for boldly declaring that Jesus is the Lord. But it is usually wiser to share what you have discovered about Jesus, because people are generally more receptive to this. Conversely, dogmatic declarations usually close the conversation down.

- *It means picking carefully what you express disagreement about.* Many Christians feel they are obligated to register disagreement over any false statement non-Christians make. Of course, if someone directly asks you, "Do you believe that all religions lead to God?" you should answer "No." But is it not wiser to focus on Jesus' invitation to receive His free gift of forgiveness than to initiate a critique of other religions? Save your disagreements for matters directly related to the gospel. Try to keep the conversation going about Jesus' offer, and avoid pushing your personal opinion about matters (like your political opinions) that are not emphasized by scripture.

- *It means refusing to become belligerent.* Paul said, "Never pay back evil for evil to anyone. Respect what is right in the sight of all men. If possible, so far as it depends on you, be at peace with all men" (Romans 12:17,18). Certainly this applies when people become argumentative, or mocking, or indulge in name-calling. As much as we may want to put such people in their place, getting down in the verbal mud with them has no place for those who follow Jesus. Responding to verbal abuse with self-control sometimes convicts the abuser's conscience (1 Peter 3:16).

- *It means humbly apologizing for wrong speech or behavior.* Who can read a passage like Colossians 3:17-4:6 without realizing that he sometimes seriously misrepresents Christ? What then? Then we have yet another opportunity to speak graciously by admitting that we were wrong.

Years ago, I was walking by my neighbor's garage while talking with a younger Christian I was discipling. Earlier that day I had foolishly dumped some waste behind his garage because I was too lazy to properly dispose of it. As we walked by his garage, my neighbor was shoveling up the waste and said, "Who would do something like this?" There was only one way for me to respond. I went over, told him I did it, asked him to forgive me, and took his shovel and cleaned up the mess. He just stood there, dumbfounded—both that I had dumped the waste and that I apologized. Years later, when he had become a Christian, he told me what an impression that incident made on him. He had been part of a legalistic religious sect at the time. "I could never have admitted I had done something like that," he said. "I knew you were a Christian, and I couldn't get over that you admitted it and apologized for it." When we admit our misdeeds, God often works through this to show people the powerful freeing effect of His grace on sinful people like us. Our apologies become an aroma of Christ that attract people toward Him!

Why is gracious speech so important? It is important *theologically* because God made each person in His image, because each person has an eternal soul, and because God loves each person enough to give His Son to die for him. Gracious speech is *practically* important because it will help us to "know how to respond to each person" (Colossians 4:6b). Gracious speech usually encourages more genuine dialogue, which helps us to learn about people's real questions and perceived needs, which in turn enables us to share more effectively how Jesus provides what they really need.

God can teach you how to be a gracious conversationalist! Tell Him that you want this, and ask Him to tutor you. Observe Christian friends who are strong in this skill. Practice conversing graciously with your Christian friends. Ask Him for opportunities to do this with non-Christians in your sphere of influence. You will see more people realize that Christianity does not turn people into mean-spirited, narrow-minded, domineering bigots. You will see more people feel safe to ask questions about Jesus. You will see more people willing to have ongoing personal and faith-related conversations. You will see more people respond to invitations to come to a Bible study and meet your Christian friends. Best of all, God will work through you to help more people find life by receiving Christ!

Chapter 18
Colossians 4:7-18
Quality Teams

Colossians 4:7 As to all my affairs, Tychicus, our beloved brother and faithful servant and fellow bond-servant in the Lord, will bring you information. [8] For I have sent him to you for this very purpose, that you may know about our circumstances and that he may encourage your hearts; [9] and with him Onesimus, our faithful and beloved brother, who is one of your number. They will inform you about the whole situation here. [10] Aristarchus, my fellow prisoner, sends you his greetings; and also Barnabas's cousin Mark (about whom you received instructions; if he comes to you, welcome him); [11] and also Jesus who is called Justus; these are the only fellow workers for the kingdom of God who are from the circumcision, and they have proved to be an encouragement to me. [12] Epaphras, who is one of your number, a bondslave of Jesus Christ, sends you his greetings, always laboring earnestly for you in his prayers, that you may stand perfect and fully assured in all the will of God. [13] For I testify for him that he has a deep concern for you and for those who are in Laodicea and Hierapolis. [14] Luke, the beloved physician, sends you his greetings, and also Demas.
[15] Greet the brethren who are in Laodicea and also Nympha and the church that is in her house. [16] When this letter is read among you, have it also read in the church of the Laodiceans; and you, for your part read my letter that is coming from Laodicea. [17] Say to Archippus, "Take heed to the

ministry which you have received in the Lord, that you may fulfill it."

[18] I, Paul, write this greeting with my own hand. Remember my imprisonment. Grace be with you. (Colossians 4:7-18)

Paul ends his letter to the Colossians in his customary way—by sending greetings from those who are with him (4:7-14), by greeting individuals among the letter's recipients (4:15), and by giving final instructions and a farewell (4:16-18). We learn in 4:7-14 that in spite of being under house arrest, Paul was personally connected with an extensive team. He mentions eight companions, and there may well have been more than that.

- Tychichus is probably the courier who brought this letter to the Colossians. He will give them more information about Paul's situation and encourage them in the Lord.

- Onesimus is a runaway slave from Colossae whom Paul is sending back to his master, Philemon (see Paul's letter to Philemon for more on this fascinating situation).

- Aristarchus is imprisoned with Paul.

- Mark, whom Paul had earlier dismissed from his team (Acts 15:37,38), receives Paul's commendation as a trusted worker.

- Jesus (also called Justus), along with Aristarchus and Mark, are Paul's only Jewish teammates.[1]

- Epaphras planted the Colossian church (and possibly the churches in nearby Laodicea and Hieropolis). He evidently brought news of the Colossian church's situation. He now remains with Paul, praying faithfully for them.

---

[1] Paul may mention this to emphasize that, contrary to the false teachers' insistence, Jewish descent is *not* a requirement of Christian spirituality.

- Luke is a doctor who has long been Paul's travelling companion. He may be with Paul to help him with his physical disabilities.

- Demas is one of Paul's teammates, but later deserted their team (see 2 Tim. 4:10).

We could learn many useful spiritual lessons by delving into each of these characters in greater detail. But instead we will focus on the fact that Paul served the Lord with a team of other Christian workers. The New Testament records over thirty people who served alongside Paul as he planted churches all over the northern Mediterranean Basin.

Christians often think of Paul as the ultimate example of a strong Christian leader, bravely traveling from city to city by himself or with maybe one companion. But this picture is completely inaccurate, maybe a projection of western Christianity's conformity to our individualistic culture. For Paul, being without other teammates was the last resort. Other Christians had to be in major crisis before he would consider being without them for even a short time.

> Therefore when we could endure it no longer, we thought it best to be left behind at Athens alone, [2] and we sent Timothy, our brother and God's fellow worker in the gospel of Christ, to strengthen and encourage you as to your faith....
> (1 Thessalonians 3:1)

Why did Paul plant churches with a team of workers? The answer seems to be connected to the nature of the church itself as the Body of Christ. Local churches are not a collection of self-sufficient islands; they are an organic union of individual Christians who have different gifts and strengths. They function and flourish best when they serve together and interdependently.

1 Corinthians 12:14 For the body is not one member, but many. [15] If the foot says, "Because I am not a hand, I am not a part of the body," it is not for this reason any the less a part of the body. [16] And if the ear says, "Because I am not an eye, I am not a part of the body," it is not for this reason any the less a part of the body. [17] If the whole body were an eye, where would the hearing be? If the whole were hearing, where would the sense of smell be? [18] But now God has placed the members, each one of them, in the body, just as He desired. [19] If they were all one member, where would the body be? [20] But now there are many members, but one body. [21] And the eye cannot say to the hand, "I have no need of you"; or again the head to the feet, "I have no need of you." [22] On the contrary, it is much truer that the members of the body which seem to be weaker are necessary; [23] and those members of the body which we deem less honorable, on these we bestow more abundant honor, and our less presentable members become much more presentable, [24] whereas our more presentable members have no need of it. But God has so composed the body, giving more abundant honor to that member which lacked, [25] so that there may be no division in the body, but that the members may have the same care for one another. [26] And if one member suffers, all the members suffer with it; if one member is honored, all the members rejoice with it. (1 Corinthians 12:14-26)

If this is what the church is, then church planters should be mobile churches. By relating to one another as a team, they can encourage one another through the rigors of the work. Their diverse spiritual gifts and strengths can be more effective when they function as teammates. They can simultaneously model this kind of "Body-life" to the churches they plant. This is probably why, although Paul was the leader of this team, he refers to the individuals in 4:7-14 not as subordinates, but as "my *fellow* bond-servant" (4:7), "my *fellow* prisoner" (4:10), and "*fellow* workers" (4:11). This emphasizes their primary identity as teammates, interdependent members of Christ's Body.

Whether we plant churches, or start new ministries in our local church, or lead home fellowship groups, we should do our best to cultivate and sustain quality teams. What do they look like? This passage gives us several features of such teams. We will focus on three of them.

Quality teams are made up of bond-servants

As to all my affairs, Tychicus, our... fellow *bond-servant* in the Lord, will bring you information... [12] Epaphras, who is one of your number, a *bondslave* of Jesus Christ, sends you his greetings... (Colossians 4:7)

The root word for "bond-servant" in 4:7 and "bondslave" in 4:12 is *doulos.* This word refers to someone who "one who gives himself up to another's will" and to one who is "devoted to another to the disregard of one's own interests."[2] Paul uses this word to refer to himself and to other Christian workers to designate "those whose service is used by Christ in extending and advancing His cause among men."[3] Joseph Tson notes that "In (21st) century Christianity we have replaced the expression... 'slave' with 'servant.' But there is an important difference. A servant *gives service* to someone, but a slave *belongs* to someone. We commit ourselves to do something, but when we surrender ourselves to someone, we give ourselves up."[4]

So quality Christian leadership teams consist of people who have given themselves up to Christ to build and care for His church even

[2] Strong, J. (2001). *Enhanced Strong's Lexicon.* Bellingham, WA: Logos Bible Software.

[3] Strong, J. (2001). *Enhanced Strong's Lexicon.* Bellingham, WA: Logos Bible Software.

[4] Quoted in Murray J. Harris, *Slave of Christ* (InterVarsity Press, 1999), p. 18.

at the expense of their own personal interests. Teams that are based on anything else—self-aggrandizement, lust for adventure, rivalrous competition, need for constant affirmation or positive results—will fall apart when things get tough. Of course, not all Christians have made such a commitment. This is why Paul laments to the Philippian Christians that:

> I have no one else (besides Timothy) of kindred spirit who will genuinely be concerned for your welfare.[21] For they all seek after their own interests, not those of Christ Jesus. (Philippians 2:20-21)

What helps us to give ourselves to God in this radical way? It is receiving and experiencing the faithfulness of God's love. John says in 1 John 4:19 that "we love because He first loved us." Paul says in Romans 12:1 that it is because of the manifold "mercies of God" that have been shown to us that we should offer ourselves up to Him. In the Old Testament God gives us a beautiful picture of how experiencing this kind of love can motivate such commitment.

> If a fellow Hebrew sells himself or herself to be your servant and serves you for six years, in the seventh year you must set that servant free. [13] When you release a male servant, do not send him away empty-handed. [14] Give him a generous farewell gift from your flock, your threshing floor, and your winepress. Share with him some of the bounty with which the Lord your God has blessed you. You shall remember that you were a slave in the land of Egypt, and the Lord your God redeemed you; therefore I command you this today. [16] It shall come about if he (your slave) says to you, "I will not go out from you," because he loves you and your household, since he fares well with you; [17] then you shall take an awl and pierce it through his ear into the door, and he shall be your servant forever. (Deuteronomy 15:12-17)

If a Hebrew became a slave to pay off a debt, God commanded that his master set him free after six years with the means to resume his life as a free man. But if he loved his master because of his kindness and justice and goodness ("since he fares well with you"), he could *willingly* pledge himself to be his master's servant for the rest of his life. The piercing of his ear marked him as a bond-slave.

Likewise, Christian leadership requires deep commitment to Christ—not commitment based on peer-pressure or guilt, but commitment based on knowing from experience that there is no better life than being in God's household and advancing His interests. This is the main difference between being a "have to" teammate and being a "get to" teammate!

Quality teams express affection to and about one another

> As to all my affairs, Tychicus, our *beloved* brother... [9] and with him Onesimus, our faithful and *beloved* brother, who is one of your number....
> [14] Luke, the *beloved* physician, sends you his greetings....
> (Colossians 4:7-19)

Members of a quality team serve God out of genuine appreciation of His love for them. They also possess genuine affection for and appreciation of one another. "Beloved" (*agapetos*) has the sense of "esteemed, dear, favorite."[5] This is what newlyweds mean when they refer to each others as their "beloved."

Christian men often have problems with Paul's open affection for the Christians with whom he worked. We seem to couple a hard-working attitude with stoic impassivity toward our co-laborers. As a

---

[5] Strong, J. (2001). *Enhanced Strong's Lexicon.* Bellingham, WA: Logos Bible Software.

new Christian, I remember being shocked and dismayed at Paul's
open affection toward the Philippian Christians:

> I thank my God in all my remembrance of you, [4] always
> offering prayer with joy in my every prayer for you all... [7]
> For it is only right for me to feel this way about you all,
> because I have you in my heart... [8] For God is my witness,
> how I long for you all with the affection of Christ Jesus.
> (Philippians 1:3-8)

"Where is the strong, tough Paul that I respect so much? Why is he
being so soft and soupy?" My reaction revealed more about my
spiritual immaturity than about weakness in Paul. He teaches us that
strength and affection go together. No one is stronger or tougher
than Jesus—and He is also tender and affectionate. We need to
endure enemies and circumstantial suffering with strength and
toughness—*and* we need to express tenderness and affection to our
friends and family and team-mates. Such expressions are crucial to
trust, and trust is essential to effective teams.

Affection is related to our feelings, but it is rooted more in our choice
than our feelings. Feelings of affection are largely the outcome of the
ongoing choice to invest personally in another person. The maxim
"Invest until you feel affection" has served me well over the years. I
used to think that expressing affection without feeling it at the time
was inauthentic. And of course, it could be—flatterers do this in
order to manipulate people. I can't turn my feelings on an off like a
light-switch. But I can choose to love another person regardless of
how I feel. And if I discern that they need affection, I can choose to
express this even though I don't feel it at that moment. This is not
fakey; it is faith in God's wise call to love others. Over time, this
choice gets easier to make, showing affection feels more enjoyable,
and I actually feel affection more often.

Notice that Paul here is not primarily expressing affection *to his team-mates*, he is expressing his affection for them *to others*. He tells the Colossians that Tychicus, Onesimus, and Luke are "beloved" by him and by other members of his team. By engaging in this kind of "good gossip," Paul both honors his team-mates and models this behavior for the Colossians. He is practicing what he teaches in another letter:

> Love each other with genuine affection, and take delight in honoring each other. (Romans 12:10 NLT)

Teammates, like spouses, sometimes think that these expressions of affection become unnecessary after doing life together for many years. "They already know that I appreciate them" is usually just a rationalization for pridefully holding back from this kind of service.

Our fallen natures are aversive to this because it puts us "under" rather than "over" others. This attitude needs to be crucified rather than obeyed! Furthermore, our chronic failure to express affection and appreciation can communicate that we take our team-mates for granted. This creates a setting in which hurt feelings and competitive urges take root to cause disunity. Conversely, generous expressions of affection and appreciation create a "buffer" that often prevents these negative feelings from taking root.

So express affection and appreciation to your team-mates, and express this about them to others. This is a simple act of love, but it bears beautiful fruit!

Quality teams prize faithfulness

> Tychicus, our beloved brother and *faithful* servant...[9]
> Onesimus, our *faithful* and beloved brother.... (Colossians 4:7, 9)

When Paul praises Tychicus and Onesimus, he doesn't talk about how spiritually gifted or charismatic or "successful" they were. He calls attention to their faithfulness. "Faithful" (*pistos*) here means persons who "are worthy of trust; who can be relied upon."[6] Faithfulness is a fruit of God's Spirit (Galatians 5:23), and this character quality (known by several synonyms and metaphors) is highly valued in the New Testament.[7]

A synonym for faithfulness is "plodding." When William Carey, the pioneer missionary to India, was being honored for his ministry, he replied:

> "If, after my removal, anyone should think it worth his while to write my life, I will give you a criterion by which you may judge of its correctness. If he gives me credit for being a plodder, he will describe me justly. Anything beyond this will be too much. I can plod. I can persevere in any definite pursuit. To this I owe everything."[8]

What a counter-cultural quality! When was the last time you saw a "plodders' award ceremony" on TV? What church markets itself as "developing plodders?" Both our culture and western Christianity value super-star celebrities, slick programs, instant gratification, short-cuts, and quick-fixes. Plodding? Not so much. But according to the Bible, the real race (living one's life for Christ) goes to plodders! And quality teams are comprised of people who prize plodding.

---

[6] Strong, J. (2001). *Enhanced Strong's Lexicon.* Bellingham, WA: Logos Bible Software.

[7] Endurance, steadfastness, and perseverance are often-used key New Testament synonyms for faithfulness. Paul's exhortations "Do not faint or grow weary," "We do not lose heart," and "I press on," all describe faithfulness in action. The New Testament's description of the Christian life as a long-distance race highlights the importance of faithfulness.

[8] Timothy George, *Faithful Witness: The Life and Mission of William Carey* (Christian History Institute, 1998), p. 16.

How can we develop into faithful plodding team-mates? At the risk
of sounding corny, here are seven "P" words that answer this
question:

- Plodders stay focused on God's *promises*. We run with
  endurance the race God has set before us by fixing our eyes
  on Jesus (Hebrews 12:2). We get renewed day by day rather
  than losing heart as we focus day by day on the unseen
  eternal provisions of God revealed through His Word
  (2 Corinthians 4:16,18). George Mueller, another faithful
  plodder, explained that this was one of the keys to his
  decades-long ministry:

  "I saw more clearly than ever, that the first great and
  primary business to which I ought to attend every day was,
  to have my soul happy in the Lord... I saw that the most
  important thing I had to do was give myself to the reading of
  the Word of God, and to meditation on it... What is the food
  of the inner man?... The Word of God; and... not the simple
  reading of the Word of God, so that it only passes through
  our minds, just as water runs through a pipe, but
  considering what we read, pondering over it, and applying it
  to our hearts." [9]

Many Christian workers do not take this priority seriously. They
think their zeal and gifting and will-power will sustain them. But
sooner or later, these things no longer sustain them, and they pay the
price of discouragement and burn-out. This is one reason why we
need to find some way of regularly meditating on God's promises.

- Plodders also stay focused on God's *priorities*. We know
  what God has commissioned us to do—to help bring people
  to faith in Christ, and to help them toward spiritual

---

[9] George Mueller, A Narrative of Some of the Lord's Dealing with George Mueller, 2 vols.
(Dust and Ashes, 2003), 1:272-273.

maturity in the context of real Christian community. This is
Christ's mission, and our lives must stay integrated around
His mission. Faithful workers do not allow the difficulties of
the work to re-define their mission into something easier.
If, when we are digging a foundation we run into a huge
boulder, we do not decide to pitch a tent instead! We may
alter our digging methods, we may adjust our construction
schedule, but we keep on digging the foundation! So we
need to periodically evaluate your actual priorities in light
of Christ's priorities, asking Him to prune and re-shape our
schedules accordingly.

- Plodders work with people *prayerfully.* Plodders are
  prayerful for those they serve because they realize that real
  change happens only by God's power, and God's power is
  unleashed by prayer. This is why Paul draws attention to
  Epaphras' prayers for the Colossians:

  Epaphras, who is one of your number, a bondslave of Jesus
  Christ, sends you his greetings, always laboring earnestly for
  you in his prayers, that you may stand perfect and fully
  assured in all the will of God. (Colossians 4:12)

Those with whom we work have past damage that we cannot heal.
They have besetting sins that we cannot overcome. They have need
of counsel that requires wisdom that we don't have. They need
repentance that we cannot elicit. They need vision that we cannot
impart. They need protection during temptation that we cannot
provide. Sooner or later, we must learn to pray regularly for people
along these lines. Much of this prayer will be short prayers as we
think about them and their needs. We do not need to counsel God on
what He needs to do; we simply need to hold them up to God and
ask Him to influence them. He will not violate their free will, but He
will answer our prayers to strongly influence them. Such prayers are

also often the context in which God grants us further insight on how we might better serve the people for whom we are praying.

- Plodders work with people *persistently.* There is no contradiction between praying for God to work and persistently doing our part. Like farmers (2 Timothy 2:6), plodders show up day after day to work hard and intentionally. Like marathon runners, plodders strive mile after mile. They keep meeting with those they disciple— week after week, month after month, year after year. They keep studying and counseling and coaching and praying. They keep issuing challenges and encouragement whenever needed. It's not fancy, and there are rarely dramatic moments—but the impact accumulates over time, and the other person often catches the vision to become a plodder discipler with others.

- Plodders work with people *patiently.* People's brokenness can go very deep, and maturity takes a long time. This is why "patience" and "forbearance" are emphasized so much in Paul's profile of Christian workers.[10] Patience (*makrothumia*) means "long-suffering" for a reason! It is the opposite of being fed up and deciding "I don't have to put up with this"—such a hypocritical attitude when the Lord has been so patient with us!

- Plodders anticipate God's *power.* Plodders can expect God's power, not necessarily to perform miracles, but to energize them to keep plodding (Colossians 1:11). When we are tired, we can ask the Lord for power to give ourselves away—and He will provide it. When we are fearful about a difficult conversation, we can ask the Lord for power to speak up—and He will give it to us. When we are

---

[10] See 2 Corinthians 6:6; Ephesians 4:2; Colossians 1:11; 3:12; 2 Timothy 3:10; 4:2.

frustrated, we can ask the Lord for the power to be
constructive—and He will give it to us. Our power is very
limited and easily runs out, but God's power is "according
to the strength of His might!"

- Plodders look forward to eventual spiritual *prosperity.*
  Plodders can expect their work to prosper over time.

Therefore, my beloved brethren, be steadfast, immovable,
always abounding in the work of the Lord, knowing that
your toil is not in vain in the Lord. (1 Corinthians 15:58)

The one who sows to the Spirit will from the Spirit reap
eternal life. [9] Let us not lose heart in doing good, for in due
time we will reap if we do not grow weary. (Galatians 6:8-9)

In ministry, we reap *what* we sow, *more* than we sow, and *later* than
we sow. Being a plodder-discipler is one key way of sowing to the
Spirit—investing our time and energy into something that the Spirit
wants to prosper. If we keep plodding instead of growing weary and
losing heart, we will reap in due time—when God grants. This
reaping includes not only people who develop as workers, but
eternal reward in the next life and deeper happiness in this life!

Canadian poet Robert Service summed up his career this way:

"In truth, I am nothing but a plodding mediocrity... Mere
mediocrity does not go very far, but a plodding one gets
quite a distance. There is joy in that success, and a
distinction can come from courage, fidelity, and industry."

How much more true this is when Christian team-mates plod
together to serve God! The distinction we will receive comes not
from men, but from God Himself: "Well done, good and faithful
servant... Enter into the joy of your Master!" (Matthew 25:23)